KiNDERGARTEN

CONCEPTION, BIRTH

AND

EARLY CHILDHOOD

CONCEPTION, BIRTH
AND
EARLY CHILDHOOD

By
NORBERT GLAS
M.D. (Vienna), L.R.C.P. (London),
M.R.C.S. (England)

ANTHROPOSOPHIC PRESS, INC.
Spring Valley, New York

Cover designed by Peter van Oordt
and produced with funding assistance
from the Cultural Freedom Fund.

Glas, Norbert.
    Conception, birth, and early childhood.

    1. Pregnancy.   2. Childbirth.   3. Infants (Newborn)—
Care and hygiene.   4. Holistic medicine. I. Title.
RG525.G5135   1983   618.2   83-15597
ISBN 0-910142-54-8

Printed in the United States of America

FOREWORD

It is indeed a joy to have Norbert Glas's *Conception, Birth and Early Childhood* again available for the thoughtful consideration and guidance of the growing number of young couples interested in giving their offspring the best possible start in this chaotic and challenging world. The author's point of view will find its resonance in the desire of many young people today for a broader and more natural view of life. Written twenty years ago for the English public, it has very little that needs correction, for he speaks of timeless and world-wide truths. It is hoped that not only the young will find it a source book of universal truths in meeting the practical problems of parenthood, but that it may be a stimulus to imaginative and reflective thinking on the part of teachers of young children, doctors and nurses to supplement their usual education. The fact that no cases of smallpox have occurred in the continental United States since 1949, for example, gives reason to discontinue the universal requirement for "vaccination." To this the author adds subtle considerations that are basically far more important.

After reading this book, all parents should be conscious of the infinite harm that occurs, and the basis for all sorts of rhythmic disturbance laid by allowing the television or radio to disturb a child's rest. The fact that the child can sleep in spite of the lights and noise in a room is a testimony to the goodness of "nature" and adjustability of "man," as well as the ignorance and insensitivity of parents that grows ever deeper.

This book should lead young parents and those who advise them to a greater sensitivity of the child's real needs and a willingness to sacrifice momentary pleasures to the future health and strength of their children.

Since this book was originally published, the Western world has become deeply involved, even engulfed, in the use of drugs to induce changes in consciousness for which the doctors must take partial responsibility. There is no space here to repeat the facts set forth elsewhere in regard to the harmful effects on health of the use of these drugs but it must be emphasized that the subtle but incisive undercutting of the will impulses by the smoking of derivatives of cannabis ("pot" and "hash") are more obvious to the educator than the psychologist, doctor and law enforcement officer. While "performance" of mechanical and superficial acts may be relatively good or even superior, there is a deep lack of motivation and "esprit de corps" that blocks the creative educator and distresses the parents. From these effects, even on the occasional users, more serious destructions occur with the other natural and synthetic hallucinogens and "hard" drugs. An aspect, insufficiently indicated, is that Rudolf Steiner has presented a path to suprasensible realities[1] that is made immeasurably more difficult by any weakening of the will, which is

---

[1] Rudolf Steiner, *Knowledge of the Higher Worlds and Its Attainment*, Anthroposophic Press, Spring Valley, N.Y.

the hallmark of drug use even without obvious dependency. The clairvoyance and higher states attainable through strengthening of the power of thought[1] and meditation[2] opens up the higher worlds to view, understanding and indwelling. Transitory drug-induced glimpses of other worlds must be seen in sharp contrast to the conscious entrance into the reality that stands behind the manifest world. One's mind turns to the words of the Good Shepherd (John 10:1).

What relation do these considerations have on the embryo and child? Any pollution of the environment of the unborn or newborn child will have much more effect on the growing organism than on the adult smoker or drug user. These harmful effects have only been partially evaluated but the sensitive reader instinctively realizes that great dangers lurk here. It cannot be too frequently emphasized that the child is a naked soul into whom, through the senses, breath and food, flow unobstructed all that is in the environment. Parents, as makers and guardians of this environment, must consciously take up the charge that the mother's body relinquishes at the moment of birth.

Henry N. Williams, M.D., D.N.B., D.H.T.

Chairman, Fellowship of Physicians, U.S.A.

Lancaster, Pa. 1972

---

[1] Rudolf Steiner, *Practical Training in Thought*, Anthroposophic Press, Spring Valley, N.Y.

[2] Frederich Rittelmeyer, *Meditation.* Available from Anthroposophic Press, Spring Valley, N.Y.

INTRODUCTION

I was once called in to see a little boy of two and a half. When I went into the sick-room, the child cried bitterly. He hated the idea of being seen by the doctor, and while I tried to talk, he struggled and resisted. His mother did her best to reassure and quiet him with promises. Finally, as a last resort, she told him that when he was grown up he should have a helicopter (at that time the most modern form of aeroplane). This promise she repeated three times.

On another occasion, I was visiting for the second time a little girl of seven, who had measles. While I was in the hall, I heard the blare of a wireless coming from her room. The mother met me with a beaming face. "Isn't it wonderful! I have put the radio in her room. She would never have stayed in bed quietly for a fortnight without it. I leave it on all day until she falls asleep, and she gives me no trouble at all."

Soon after this I had to go and see a boy of five who had a cough. I had some difficulty in finding the house, and went in with that feeling of satisfaction at having found it at last, which only doctors in country practices will understand. But my complacency was soon shattered. A little boy suddenly rushed towards me holding a pistol in his hand. "I'm going to shoot you," he announced briefly as he took aim. He pressed the trigger, and disappeared as suddenly as he had come, satisfied, no doubt, with his brilliant attack.

Finally, a father complained to me recently about his little girl of four. He was afraid that she might be backward. When I asked what were the symptoms which drove him to this conclusion he said: "Well, for instance she takes no interest in television. I put it on for her—the children's program, of course—and she simply doesn't give a hoot for it."

When one has many such experiences as these, one gradually comes no longer to see the funny side of them. And it is borne in upon one how great is the influence which the trends of modern life have upon man from his childhood on. From the medical point of view it is necessary to make it quite clear how great are the dangers of these trends, which undermine the health of the people from childhood on into later life.

The statement has been made by a high school teacher at a public lecture in a pedagogical institution, that many schools have actually to face epidemics of thefts, frauds and lying. And whom do the teachers accuse? The parents of the children.

CONTENTS

CONCEPTION, BIRTH

AND

EARLY CHILDHOOD

I

CONCEPTION

I

Only through a new understanding of the human being can a remedy be found for many of the diseases which have their origin in the way of life from earliest childhood. I shall therefore try, in this book, to show how parents, teachers, doctors and nurses should learn to look at the development of man in a different way from that which they are at present taught in schools, universities and hospitals.

In order to present this new point of view, it will be necessary to refer to the teaching of Rudolf Steiner, upon which it is based. This I shall always do briefly and only in so far as is necessary for the understanding of the child.

II

One idea, fundamental to this book, is that the human being is not created merely by father and mother, but exists already

3

before birth and conception. He exists as an individual, in a spiritual form, in a world that is not physically visible.

Man, striving for incarnation, chooses in his parents, the human beings with whose help it becomes possible for him to live on earth. In ancient times, the mother was deeply connected with the coming child, even before conception. She lived in a dream-like world and experienced much of the supersensible realm in her feeling-life.

In fairy tales, we often find the coming of a child announced by all kinds of beings. In Grimm's story—"The Carnation"—an angel appears to the Queen and prophesies for her a son who will have everything he wants. In "Sleeping Beauty" the frog announces to the Queen that before a year has passed she will give birth to a daughter. And it is said that the mother of Alexander the Great, and also his father, both had remarkable dreams before their son was born.*

In the appearance of the Angel who prophesies to Mary the coming of the Jesus child we see the archetypal annunciation. We can understand then, why it was that many great painters, such as Fra Angelico, and others, so often painted the Annunciation. Although real spiritual vision was becoming rare in those times people still had a deep religious feeling for the great events on earth. Through these beautiful pictures it was intended that men should experience how the highest Being was

---

* The night before the consummation of their marriage, Olympias dreamed that a thunderbolt fell upon her body, which kindled a great fire, whose divided flames dispersed themselves all about, and then were extinguished. And Philipp, sometime after he was married, dreamt that he sealed up his wife's body with a seal, whose impression, as he fancied, was the figure of a lion. He was told by Aristander of Telmerrus the meaning of his dream was, that the Queen was with child of a boy, who would one day prove as stout and courageous as a lion. (See Plutarch's *Lives, Alexander.*)

announced to his mother on earth. At the same time they knew—perhaps only half-consciously—that in these pictures something lives that has its importance for every human being even if, at the human level, there is but a feeble reflection of it. For everyone came originally to his mother. Not everyone was announced in such a miraculous way, but each had been guided by an Angel who protected him, at least at the beginning of his life. In those days of the famous painters, such feelings had a great reality.

Even in our days there are women who have seen their child in a dream long before its birth, and have been quite amazed when they saw that the real child was exactly like the dream-picture.

III

Such cases of the prophetic annunciation of a child have come to seem strange to people of the present day. The last echoes of such an annunciation may perhaps be recognised in a woman's sudden longing for a child. A feeling of this kind may arise in a delicate way, and can easily be veiled by instincts and passions. A subtle awareness should of course be able to distinguish between mere passion and the real call of a child.

As soon as the mother knows that she is going to have a child, a solemn feeling should awaken in her that she has been given an important task. She should have a feeling of devoted expectation toward the child from the beginning, and no egotistic wish or desire. An attitude, in fact, perhaps most comparable to that which a really religious person had, in olden times, when he opened himself to the working of the Divine

Will. The higher being could then speak through this human soul who had renounced all his own personal wishes. This feeling of devotion must be free from any sentimentality. In practice, such a demand means to the father and mother that they should for instance free themselves from the wish that the coming child may be a boy or a girl; this they should leave to the will of the incarnating being. Nor should the decision to have a child ever be ruled by the idea that the baby will give a meaning to the marriage; or by a suggestion of the doctor that it might be a help to the woman to have children; these considerations are only due to human egotism. The question, on the other hand, as to why any woman should be unable to have a child, is even more complicated in our time. But before discussing this, it must be pointed out that a child does not only choose his parents, but also wishes to be born at some special time.

Great personalities, such as Goethe, were convinced that the constellation under which a man is born has a great influence on his destiny. I shall mention, further on, what Goethe has to say about his own constellation at the time of his birth. Some of the great astronomers were convinced astrologers. Unfortunately, through dilettantism, astrology has been brought, by lack of understanding and superstition, into a well-merited disrepute. All this does not alter the fact, however, that there is a close connection between human life and the positions of the stars. How otherwise would it have been possible, for instance, for Tycho de Brahe to predict the death of the Sultan from the constellation of the stars?

In order to prevent misunderstanding, it must be emphasized that I do not wish in this book to recommend the practice of birth control in accordance with the star-constellations. Centuries ago, some philosophers had such ideas; one of them was Thomas Campanella, who wrote of a utopia, *The State of the Sun*. In this work, it is suggested that the birth of children should be fixed in accordance with favorable constellations in the heavens. This is not the place to deal with the question as to why such books have been written; I only wish to point to the fact that such writers and philosophers were fully convinced of the influence of the stars on man.

IV

It is clear, from the preceding section, that parents should listen inwardly, in order to discover when their child should come to them. They will only find out if they can hear the call. But it frequently happens that under present day conditions, the more delicate feelings cannot awaken in the soul. In these days, it has become usual to fix the time for the coming of children according to "practical" ideas; whether, for instance, the parents have the right kind of house, or a big enough flat; whether the man has enough income, and so forth. The author is fully aware that many arguments can be brought forward to show that birth control is important and right from economic and social aspects. He does not intend to discuss this, nor the Roman Catholic attitude to these problems. The child alone will be taken into consideration; the child who wants to come to his parents at a special time from the spiritual world. This being will have no understanding, of course, of earthly reasoning, but will feel any resistance or opposition to its coming.

It can be much worse even, if a child who is already conceived is not wanted by its chosen parents. It is not easy to follow the destiny of such unwanted children into later life. Also it is not perhaps possible to see in our experiences of these people, an outward proof that their unwantedness was the cause of their misfortunes. But one can and should try to make some investigation into their lives.

One example may be mentioned. A man and a girl formed a quite superficial relationship. They hardly thought of marriage, and before the woman knew that she was pregnant, they had already separated. For both, therefore, the child was definitely an unwanted one. After a few months, however, the girl had become reconciled to her condition. She had come to persuade herself that she must assume the responsibility for her deed, and she thus became used to and familiar with the idea of becoming a mother. In the end, she could look forward to the birth of her child with kindly feelings. Just as she had reached this stage, a premature birth took place unexpectedly and the child died a few hours later.

Another case may be mentioned—that of a man, whose coming to earth, according to his parents, was not desired. It was the mother who did not want him. This man's destiny was difficult from the beginning. Not only did he suffer from various ailments, but he always felt himself to be a stranger—not at home. This may have been the reason why he always longed to go to other countries. He loved to learn other languages and to talk to foreigners. When he grew up his mind was deranged for many years.

Such histories are not easily found out, because the people concerned fortunately do not know that they were unwanted, and the parents are not usually willing to discuss such a question with their now grown-up children. If a representative collection of the histories of such people were made, it could be very instructive. Only then would an investigation that has been carried out recently have a real moral value. This research was concerned with the problem of the unwanted child, and was made for statistical reasons. It shows that there are unwanted children in many families. In Goethe's novel, *Elective Affinities*, the problem has an important place. In this wonderful story, a child is born who, through the strange destinies of the adults, must be considered an unwanted one. Goethe therefore lets the child die in early life through a mysterious accident. One would perhaps have a better understanding of the lives of many people who have special difficulties if one realized that they had been unwanted. Such a person bears a special stamp of misery or disharmony in his fate under which he has to suffer all through life.

An interesting article in the British Medical Journal, is worth mentioning here.* Acrodynia is an illness of early childhood. The children lose their appetite, sleep badly, are moody and want to be carried about. Their hands become purplish, their arms and legs limp, their pulse is accelerated, and they perspire. Feet and hands are cold. This strange disease is not frequent, but one comes across it from time to time. What is of great interest for us here is the following fact. Four of the six cases described were unwanted children. One child, for instance, was conceived while the parents were only engaged, and the two grandmothers were afraid of the scandal in their respectable families. The second

---

* *A Psychiatric Study of Six Cases of Infantile Acrodynia*, Duncan Leys, M.D. and Kenneth Camaon, M.B., 1952.

one was the result of a failure in birth control, and so was the third. The fourth had come against the will of the mother, who had already borne six children.

V

In complete contrast to the unwanted child is that being who has been forced into existence by artificial insemination. This kind of conception could only have become possible in an age when many people have lost the feeling of respect for human destiny. The reason why the practice of artificial insemination must be rejected becomes obvious from this book. That section should be recalled in which I spoke of the waiting of the children themselves for the right time for conception. No account is taken here of religious or social traditions, nor of legal arguments. It will be necessary to investigate the lives of such "artificial" men. But it must be many years before this can be done since artificial insemination has not long been in practice. According to a report in the Swiss Medical Journal (Schweizer Medizinische Wochenschrift 1950, 80, 667) Professor E. Anderes has said that during the last few years about 15,000–20,000 artificial impregnations have been accomplished yearly in America, and about 6,000 in London.

VI

To sum up what has been said about the time of conception, I would draw attention especially to that feeling of selfless devotion that is the ideal attitude of the mother towards the coming child. The answer of Mary to the proclaiming Angel most perfectly expresses this ideal attitude. "Behold the handmaid of the Lord; be it unto me according to thy word." (St. Luke i, 38).

The author knows that this demand on the mother is an ideal one. Man, however, is free to strive for it. May every mother find her way to it, with the help and support of the father.

II

PREGNANCY

I

Many women suffer, during the first three months of pregnancy, from all kinds of disagreeable disturbances. These may be both mental and physical.

The trouble may be morning sickness, which can become so bad that there is an aversion to all food. There is usually an unbalanced and changeable state of mind. Depression, and an inclination to weep are frequent. There may be a great sensitivity toward sense impressions, as, for example, odors. Giddiness and fainting-fits give a feeling of mental and bodily uncertainty and weakness. These symptoms, well-known to the layman as well as to the doctor, are the picture of a special condition connected with the first three months of pregnancy, as all earthly events are pictures of spiritual happenings. It has been recommended above that the pregnant woman should have an attitude of selfless devotion toward her child. In her soul, she has the possibility of developing such an attitude if she keeps her mind open to the heavens from which the child is coming. But as far as her body is concerned, a difficult situation arises. She is forced to provide, in her body, the place where her child is to live for nine months. In the beginning of pregnancy it is as if there were all the time a slight physical conflict between the developing embryo, and the mother, who up to the moment of conception, has lived as an individual being in her own body. Thus the body as well as the soul has to come to the right degree of selflessness in order to make way for the child. The latter to a certain extent dislodges the being of the mother from her body. At first the mother feels this interference with her organism a great deal, and suffers from it. But as soon as she becomes used to it, which happens after the first three months, she can gain much in a spiritual way. She has more connection now with the heavenly forces than before pregnancy, because her mind has become slightly detached from her body. So she has the possibility of soul-experiences of a higher order than in her life apart from pregnancy. She should try to listen more and more to what speaks to her inwardly. In this way she comes to a closer connection with the child, and realizes how far away it still is in the supersensible world. She may experience beautiful dream-pictures that only need a true interpretation for their understanding.

II

It is important rightly to picture the condition of pregnancy. The soul and spirit of the woman are to a certain extent displaced from her physical body, and she becomes thereby more connected with the heavens; the child, on the other hand, is descending from the spiritual world and gradually shaping its earthly body. The mother thus gains, during her pregnancy, a growing relationship to, and a closer understanding for the realms from which her child is coming down. This is the true reason for the great change that can be observed in the pregnant woman; she can become wiser and gain in knowledge. She should recognize how she is lifted up from the ordinary course of life, and is thereby given the possibility of devoting herself to the new task. One can understand, then, why it is that Rudolf Steiner has recommended that women, when pregnant, should absorb themselves in the contemplation of Raphael's pictures of Mary with the Child. This great painter has shown in the most beautiful way how the divine Mother looks upwards from the earth to the stars to receive the Holy Child whose Being rays down from the region of the sun. Mary thus reveals the child to man on earth. These paintings are not only beautiful; they are also the right food for the soul of a mother-to-be. Healing strength flows from the colors and the gestures in these pictures. Nowadays, people have to be enlightened before they can realize the wealth there is for everybody in such treasures of art.

III

At present, it is difficult for the pregnant woman to achieve such a mood. The public welfare service for pregnant women has become a routine affair, concerned mainly with physical health. There are two different methods that are suggested to women as a preparation for birth, and to make easier the event; sometimes both are combined. One method aims at the utmost strengthening of the muscles by exercises and massage. This procedure must be rejected if one considers fully, from the point of view from which this book is written, what happens in pregnancy and birth. Nearly all powerful massage and gymnastics harden the muscles and this is just the opposite of what is brought about by the natural processes of the body. The body should, indeed, become softer, more pliant and flexible, for the growing embryo. An ordinary healthy way of living, with all the movements and actions that come about naturally, should be enough.

The other method adopts specialized gymnastics for pregnant women. Relaxation exercises have become the fashion. These are often combined with breathing exercises originating from old Eastern rituals. In this way the body may become more flexible than is desirable. The child has then too much space, and does not experience the resistance it should have for its natural development.

(Despite all this it cannot be denied that both methods have their advantages in all cases with complications, but here we are thinking of the average woman who is given advice according to the routine in the antenatal clinics of maternity hospitals).

IV

For the woman with a normal course of pregnancy, no more should be done than the exercise usual in a healthy person leading an ordinary everyday life. Moving the limbs in the way that is necessary for walking and not too heavy work, is all that is recommended. Food should be chosen such as is good for a healthy woman—fresh, unboiled milk, fresh vegetables— steamed, not spoilt by boiling for a long time—salads, fruit and brown bread. Dishes containing much fat, salt, or high seasoning should, of course, be avoided, and also tea and coffee;

as the child is sensitive to nicotine, the pregnant woman must not smoke. On the other hand, if she is healthy, she should certainly not, as is unfortunately so often done "as a precaution," be given strong medicines merely because this is a routine practice in the welfare clinics. In some of these clinics every patient is given a preparation of iron, cod liver oil or special vitamins without any discrimination as to individual needs. It is accepted without question that in any case they can do no harm!

Such light remedies as will make the birth easier may be taken as, for instance, the homeopathic dilution of Pulsatilla D 6, the dose being 5 drops, twice daily from the 5th to the 7th month, and three times daily up to the time of birth. During the last two months, it is advisable to rub copper ointment into the perineal region, and during the ninth month a daily sitzbath containing limeflower tea—ten minutes for the first three weeks, and five minutes only for the last week—is recommended. A cup of elderberry tea may also be given daily during the last month. Aschner, the well-known gynecologist, advises two or three cups of blackberry or raspberry leaf tea for the last four weeks.

Of great importance also is a preparation in so far as the inner life is concerned; this has been mentioned in previous paragraphs. Contemplation of the representations of the Virgin by Raphael should become a regular habit. Such a picture brings the future mother more easily into contact with the world of the child she is expecting. On the other hand, she should avoid the cinema, the radio and television. The reason for this lies in the fact that all these entertainments of modern times disconnect the human being from his spiritual origin.

The following instances may be specially mentioned. Women, when they are pregnant can become more open to the world of dreams and, in this way, true revelations may come to them. Yet, how can this happen if she who wants to bring back a picture from her dreams or listen again to the words that resounded in her sleep, is "cheered up" on awakening by the radio program! No human being who is interested in an inner development should be exposed to the noise of the radio first thing in the morning. Whatever experience one can bring out of sleep, and it may be only the feeling of being refreshed, is simply destroyed by the radio. A pregnant woman least of all should allow herself to be exposed to such an influence.

In the evening an expectant mother should surround her child with loving thoughts. She should have that feeling of selfless devotion I described earlier, and it is difficult to foster such a mood when scraps of impressions from a television play or a film are still dancing in front of her eyes. Finally, there is no need to discuss the evil effects of falling asleep to the noise of the radio at night.

Some women gain, during pregnancy, a much better understanding for the beauty in nature. A love for flowers and animals may arise. Such feelings should be encouraged and cultivated. We find represented in some of the pictures of the Virgin this connection of Mary and the Child with plants and animals. Think only of the "Madonna im Rosenhag" by Stefan Lochner, or Dürer's water color of the Virgin with its charming animals.

V

It is remarkable that women who would otherwise never experience such feelings and imaginations become open to them during the time they are pregnant. Sometimes it is as if the woman were surrounded by a radiant light—just because she now lives nearer to the heavenly world. It becomes possible for her now, during the day, to connect herself consciously with the world from which her child is coming down. As for her hands, they could not be better occupied than in sewing and knitting for the baby.*

Observation of the pregnant woman shows that the above-mentioned connection with a higher world develops gradually. It then remains unchanged for a time and finally grows less and less. In the first three months she feels the change in her body so strongly that she is not so open to the spiritual change. Only later does she become as it were transparent to the light the child brings down from the higher realm. This is the most attractive time of pregnancy. Towards the seventh month there is again another change. This is the time when the child has achieved the most important part of its physical development. As the child becomes more and more earthly, so the mother feels more and more her own heaviness. Her legs become unsure in their balance and soon get tired. She is now able only with an effort to carry her body upright and to move forward. In this last and most difficult time before birth the pregnant woman should try to hold to all that she gained from the middle period, which seems to be the most blessed one.

VI

The consideration in this way of the three stages of pregnancy gives a clue as to why the time of most danger is during the first,

---

* Rudolf Steiner once especially mentioned that skeins of wool should be wound, not always in the same direction, but rather alternately, clockwise and then anti-clockwise, since the one-sided movement could have a bad influence on the position of the child's umbilical cord.

and again the last three months. Up to the end of the third month, the embryo is very much exposed to the risk of expulsion from the womb, and from the seventh month on, to the possibility of a premature birth. These untimely births, however, are rare in comparison with those that take place normally.

The great connection that exists between the stars and the developing embryo has already been mentioned. In considering the human form, we must take into account the relationship between the forming of the head, chest, and limbs on the one hand, and the constellations of the zodiac on the other. In ancient times, when people were still familiar with such knowledge, this relationship was expressed by writing the sign of the Ram against the forehead, and the sign of the Fishes against the feet. The whole being of man was thus fitted into those twelve constellations of the zodiac through which circle the sun, moon and planets. It makes, of course, a great difference whether the influence of the stars is experienced from within the mother or from outside her. Before birth, the forces of the stars work on the form of the child when it is surrounded by the embryonic membranes and by the mother's body. After birth, having cast off its coverings, the newborn baby is exposed directly to these forces. This moment of birth is one of great importance for the child. It is a completely new situation, like the change from a bud to a blossom. Something new is created.

It is important to know that the individuality, in coming down to the parents, strives to be born under a constellation he has already chosen.

In our times, many people will consider such a statement fantastic. Great personalities, however, have been much concerned with the problem of the stellar influences. It is impressive to read Goethe's ideas about his own birth constellation. "On the 28th of August, 1749, at mid-day, as the clock struck twelve, I came into the world at Frankfort-on-the-Main. My horoscope was propitious. The sun stood in the sign of the Virgin and had culminated for the day; Jupiter and Venus looked on him with a friendly eye, and Mercury not adversely; while Saturn and Mars kept themselves indifferent; the Moon alone, just full, extended the power of her reflection all the more as she had then reached her planetary hour. She opposed herself, therefore, to my birth, which could not be accomplished until this hour was passed."

It is quite clear from these words that Goethe was convinced that the child who was about to be born—(himself)—waited for the hour of the constellation under which he wanted to enter this world.

How much one would like to recommend to the modern obstetrician to give heed to such thoughts. Science and medicine have forgotten how to take into account the influence of the heavens on man. It is to be wished that scientists and doctors might have more veneration for the occurrences of nature than many show at present. From the point of view from which this book is conceived, no attempt should ever be made to speed up a birth unless it is absolutely necessary for medical reasons. Disturbances will be brought into the life of the individual if he is born at a time other than the chosen one.

The following history of a boy may well give cause for thought to doctors. At five years old, the child, though physically well-developed gave the impression of being mentally only one and a half. He could not speak but uttered short sounds that had more an animal than a human character, and he had fits of violent rage, which it was not easy to control. It seemed to be difficult to bring about any improvement in his condition. The case-history showed that the child was backward from birth, though nothing abnormal was known, either in the mother's or the father's family. The history of the pregnancy however is interesting. The mother had no troubles at all, but a difference of opinion arose as to when the birth should be due. When the doctor was sure that the time had come, the midwife thought that the child would not be born for another two or three weeks. The authority of the doctor was accepted. Nobody seems to have been interested in what the patient thought or felt. She was perfectly well, and there were no symptoms to suggest that anything was wrong with the child. Now what happened? On the doctor's order, an anesthetic was given and the birth artificially induced. Thus there can be no doubt that the time of the child's birth was quite other than it would have been without the doctor's interference. It is surely significant that the child became backward. Similar cases should be thoroughly investigated.

How little thought is generally given to the importance of the time at which a birth takes place could be shown in many examples. I shall only mention two. Some time ago, a woman who was expecting a baby asked her doctor if he would induce the birth artificially. Her husband was coming home from the army on a certain date and she very much wanted everything to be over by the time he arrived. Another doctor thought he should make things easier for his patient. Although this woman had had a completely natural confinement a few years before, he suggested that the child should be made to come some weeks before it was due. He did not intend to use instruments, but instead advised traveling long distances in jogging buses. This method failed, and so he ordered daily hot baths. When this also had no success, he gave drastic purgatives. For a week after this attempt the woman felt ill and miserable, whereas before she had been perfectly healthy and had had no complaints. So she gave up all treatment and let the baby come in its own time. It arrived punctually and without any complications, in spite of the doctor's endeavors.

III

BIRTH

I

Although hospitals are so thoroughly equipped and hygienically well-planned, the right place for a normal confinement is in the home, for only at home can the right preparations be made to receive the child. The cradle, or Moses basket, with its blankets arranged by the mother, provides for the newborn baby a surrounding very different from the impersonal equipment of a maternity home or hospital. There is nothing to be said against such institutions as far as the blessings of cleanliness go. But unfortunately, in them, the tendency to put human beings into uniforms has taken hold. The idea of making people all alike is in a way no less of a danger than was, in past centuries, the lack of knowledge of the sources of infectious disease.

How much more intimate an experience it is for a woman to lie in her own bed for her confinement, rather than be taken to hospital in an ambulance, and there be prepared as if for an operation. (This latter is, of course, quite justifiable in some cases.)

If she goes into hospital, she leaves her usual surroundings—those into which the child chose originally to be born. Also, the feeling of expectation has for a woman something mysterious and sacred about it, in spite of a certain anxiety that some may feel. But in the midst of the routine work of a maternity hospital, it is difficult to preserve the holy mood that can prevail at home.

II

At the present moment, the subject of painless birth is much in the minds of many people. The question has arisen as to whether a woman in labor should not be given a general anesthetic. She could then give birth to her child in a somnolescent state without any pain. In England, this question gave rise to so much feeling that it was actually discussed in the House of Commons. The excitement was aroused by the social and political, rather than the moral aspect of the problem. It was feared on some sides that for economic reasons, one part of the population might have to be deprived of participation in this particular blessing of modern scientific achievement. (I only mention this as a reminder that the problem of painless birth is for many people by no means a matter of indifference.)

It has happened recently that many doctors have proposed the use of hypnotism as an anesthetic in childbirth. Thirty years ago this method was tried and praised in Germany—and then forgotten. In America also, it became fashionable twenty years ago, and is still frequently practiced, and the writer of an article in the British Medical Journal of the 5th April, 1952 seems to be satisfied with his results. There can be no doubt that it is possible to exert a hypnotic influence on the woman in labor, and many experiments have proved that painlessness can be achieved in this way. But our problem here is quite a different one. We must ask the question, "Is hypnotism a method that should be used at all in child-birth?" It is undoubtedly so that through hypnosis parts of the human soul and ego are withdrawn from the physical body. The hypnotized subject comes to a great extent under the influence of the hypnotist, and so does not any longer act out of his own will. My own experience is that the more frequently any one patient is hypnotized, the easier it becomes to bring him or her under hypnotic control. This alone seems to prove that the patient is somehow weakened in himself by hypnotism.

In the above-mentioned article, the obstetrician stresses the fact that the pregnant woman is already by nature easier to influence than if she were not pregnant. So that in any case she becomes a favorable subject for hypnosis. This is readily understood in the light of our conception of pregnancy, for in that condition the individuality of the mother is slightly displaced from her body by the child. This is a natural condition, but can it be thought right that anyone should be under the influence of another will, just in such an important moment of human existence as is the birth of a child?

It is interesting to learn how the treatment is carried out. The hypnosis is not practiced once only. It starts from four to six weeks before the birth. According to necessity a woman may have to be hypnotized four, five—even eleven times before the time when she comes into labor. As now-a-days nobody wants to waste time, doctors have decided to do, after short individual sessions, a kind of "mass-hypnosis" of groups of about six women.

Think now of how important is the experience of the birth of her child to any woman, and then of how two medical authors, who are great advocates of the hypnotic method, deal with the event. During the time of preparation, they give special post-hypnotic commands, and the most important command is that the woman shall have no recollection whatsoever of the whole happening—namely of the birth and its pains.

Then it will be easy to understand why hypnosis cannot be recommended from the standpoint of this book. Who, having this point of view, can think it desirable that another should be given power over our inner life? Who should want to bury such an important moment of our life in oblivion?

III

This problem is connected with the development of mankind, and for this reason we have to go far back for an explanation of it. Before man could gain a solid footing on earth, he lived a more spiritual existence—what could be called, in the words of the Bible, his existence in Paradise. The powers of temptation drove him forth out of the supersensible realm into the earthly sensible realm. This is referred to in the Bible as the Fall of Man. A universal guilt of mankind is here indicated as distinct from an individual one. Everyone knows these words from the Old Testament: "I will greatly multiply thy sorrow and thy conception; in sorrow thou shall bring forth children. . . ." (Genesis 3, xvi).

There can be no doubt that every individual man repeats in himself the first Fall of Man. Love in its ideal form is something purely spiritual (or Paradisal). The Tempter in the soul, working on the instincts and passion, has driven man into earthly desires. But through this he can at the same time open a gateway for the spirit by which the child can enter. Thus, one might also say that the appearance of the child is to be considered as a redemption of the preceding guilt. The child can awaken that selfless love in the parents that is essential for the activity of the true spirit.

The reader will forgive this incursion into a realm that might seem to belong rather to a religious theme. But the above conception has a practical and even a medical application also. Every woman who is to give birth to a child should understand this inner and deeper import of the event. Of course, she cannot, without some spiritual preparation, be expected suddenly to understand everything in the moment of the child's birth. But regular meditation on such a picture as the Sistine Madonna can help in the understanding of the fact of birth, at least in the feeling-life of the mother-to-be. It is for this reason that Rudolf Steiner recommended that she should occupy her mind during pregnancy, and also after the birth, with these pictures of the Virgin and Child.

From medical experience it may be emphasized that these pictures have a great strength in themselves that is transmitted to the expectant mother. Also, in her pain, the suffering woman can feel something of the higher meaning of what she is going through.

In our time, people usually object to the idea of any connection between pictures and ideas. The language of symbols with an inner truth is almost an unknown one at present. Yet the right picture can be for us the revelation of such a great mystery as we must consider the birth of man to be.

At the time of conception, man and woman sink more deeply into earthly existence. But after nine months, the woman can experience in her pains something like a redemption of her "fall." At the first sight of her child, a mother feels as if the sufferings she has just endured were already wiped out.

In truth, women should have a great longing to experience the birth of a child as consciously as possible. Then only can they take part personally in an event of mankind that concerns each one of us.

IV

Such ideas as these may appear strange, or they may be thought to have, in the best sense, a theoretical interest only. But I myself believe that they have a deep meaning for practical and everyday life. An understanding of such thoughts may, for example, lead to the opinion that anesthetics or hypnosis, which aim at achieving unconsciousness and painlessness, had better not, as a general rule, be applied in childbirth. (For any operation, of course, such as the use of forceps, nothing can be said against the blessings of anesthesia.)

The use of narcosis in birth is an intervention that can be considered in two ways. On the one hand, the woman is deprived of the possibility of experiencing the birth fully and consciously, and this applies not only to the pain, but also to the arrival of the child. The mother has a right to hear the first cry, which is like a miracle. How often has that sound been accepted by a woman with a special smile that has extinguished all the traces of suffering from her face.

On the other hand, the doctor often intervenes by the use of narcosis in a way that has a great bearing on the life of the child. There can be no doubt that the use of a general anesthetic disturbs the natural timing of the birth. This holds good, I think, for all drugs, from the old chloroform, which is still favored by many doctors, to Pethidine. If we remember what has been said about the choosing, by the child itself, of the right time, according to a particular constellation, then the objection to the universal application of anesthetics in childbirth is clearly justified.

Yet it sometimes occurs that a busy obstetrician, who is not concerned with such ideas, will use a forceps merely in order to finish off a birth more quickly and so be able to attend another woman.

V

Now what happens after birth to mother and child? Because of the pains during birth and the last weeks of pregnancy, the woman becomes aware of her body. Now at last she has brought the child to earth. The child, on the other hand, is now deprived of its natural sheaths, and, in the sense of the physical body, has become bare and naked. It needs every protection from outside so that its spiritual being can form a body that will become the right instrument for the life on earth. In one moment, almost, the little body is exposed to the outside world. This last includes the near and the more distant surroundings—that is, the room in which the birth takes place, the house, the country, and finally the given constellation in the heavens. This question has been touched on before; here it is repeated in order to make clearer what it means and what importance has the birth constellation. The following comparison may give, through a picture, an understanding of the influence that its whole surroundings have on a newborn baby. Think of this little body, of which the individual has to make its dwelling place, as being like a hollow vessel void of air. Now just as with a sealed globe holding a vacuum the air is sucked in the moment there is an opening, so does the child's body inhale all the influences of its surroundings with its first breath. This happens most intensely with those forces to which the child has the closest relationship, and to these belong especially the influence of the stars at the moment of birth. This influence may give rise to a power that prevails throughout the whole life. The mother, of course, is also closely related to the child; she has surrounded it for nine months. A new connection now starts after birth. During pregnancy, the invisible part of the mother has been to some extent removed out of her earthly body. After birth it has again gradually to enter into the body. This takes a few weeks only; some details of it will be mentioned later. After the delivery, the soul of the mother becomes as well able to surround the baby as did her body before. For this reason, the child should remain close to the mother after birth.

No woman, guided by her instincts and natural feelings, would ever dream of allowing her child to be separated from her after the confinement. Unfortunately, this happens at present in nearly all maternity homes.

VI

Consider now, without prejudice, how misguided is the procedure in these homes. In a big room stand the little cots, side by side in a long row. In each one lies a newborn baby. Separated from this ward is another or several more rooms where the mothers are. It is considered ideal if no sound from the children can reach the mothers in their department. The grown-ups, who have met here by mere chance, have not much connection with each other, but they have to be together. The children have no relationship to their neighbors, but they are in urgent need of their mothers' protection. Each helpless mother is at the mercy of a more or less friendly nurse, who usually considers it a special favor to bring her her baby at any other than the feeding time. Not to mention the fathers, who are regarded as the greatest nuisances, much better locked out. At the best, they are allowed in twice a day to see their child for a few minutes. In many hospitals with modern equipment, they are only allowed to peep at the baby through a window.

Mother and child—their archetype is the Madonna—belong together as a unity. This is a spiritual reality and should not be imposed upon by the "practical" arrangements of homes and hospitals.

VII

A modern mother—and modern is meant in the sense of the development of humanity that is right for our time—can experience something completely new after the birth is over. Her body has undergone a great revolution during the time of

31

pregnancy in order to become the physical frame for the child. Some of her organs have become much heavier. After the confinement a quick reabsorption takes place. The speed of this process can be judged from a few facts. At the time of birth, the womb weighs about 2,000 grams (over 4 lbs.). It shrinks so quickly that six weeks later the uterus has a weight of 50–60 grams (about 2 oz.). That is, for this one organ, a daily loss in weight of about 70 grams distributed over one and a half months, which is roughly double the weight that an average healthy baby gains in a day.

The reabsorption and loss of weight of some of the organs in the mother is a part of the whole condition in the first weeks after birth. This period is an important one in the life of a woman. It is essential that she should be given time enough for the change, so that no disturbance takes place while it is going on. Meanwhile, in her soul, she should seek to gain the new connection with the child that has become necessary. Now that the close bodily tie is loosened, the mother can perhaps more easily awake in her mind towards the child. Just that loosening of the child from her body leads, in many women, to a trying experience. The closest physical contact with the child that is now left to the mother consists in the feeding of it. Finding the new relationship may mean for some mothers a kind of crisis that can last up to the third month after the confinement. The avoidance of all haste will be a great help in this difficult time.

The woman should remain quietly in bed until she feels really stronger in herself. The 10–14 days usual in the past, may, in uncomplicated cases be enough. If necessary, more time may be given, but to shorten the time is certainly a mistake. Unfortunately, it has become usual in these days to make the mother get up much earlier—even sometimes after 36 hours, as has been done in America. It needs time for the different changes to take place in the body, and it can only cause harm to shorten the period of childbed. Patience is necessary if one is not to bring about damage to the organism, which will show itself in later life.

If full advantage is taken by the mother of the time after the birth, these can be most fruitful days of self-communion for her; she can now see her future task quite clearly. Any impatience in her or coming from her surroundings is disturbing and full of harm for the future.

IV

COMING INTO THE WORLD

I

At the moment of birth the child loses its embryonic coverings and the maternal envelopment. It is exposed now to the forces of gravity. A baby is usually born head first, because the head is, in its specific gravity, the heaviest part of the body.

As regards the child's head, it is remarkable that here is a meeting of two principles that seem to be contrary to one another. On the one hand, the head of the newly born is the heaviest and most material part. On the other, it has the spherical form that shows the working of cosmic laws and forces.* The process of birth can be experienced as a conversa-

---

* Rudolf Steiner expressed this on one occasion as follows: "Man, in fact, has his head formed from out of the heavens. For all the forces that work between death and a new life are in truth directed towards the shaping of his head. Although the head has to go the way of physical birth and physical inheritance—man really receives his head from Heaven. The rest of him he gets from the earth. This means that, as to the shape of his body, man is a product of Uranos and Gaea; in so far as the head is concerned, he is the result of heavenly forces; in so far as concerns his body, the result of earthly forces—Uranos and Gaea."—Rudolf Steiner, *The Riddle of Man*, not yet translated.

34

tion between these two forces—the earthly and the cosmic. The head in its beautiful form, which originates from beyond the earth, usually becomes modified because of its heaviness and size, and the narrowness of the birth passages in the mother. Its sides are pressed together in places—more in a difficult, less in a "normal" birth. The real moment of coming into the world is that moment in which the child's body—and especially its head—is pushed through the maternal pelvis. One speaks of the necessity of the head being modelled before it can leave the mother's body, and we find an especially beautiful shape of head if these forces of pressure do not have to come into play. This condition is most perfectly realized only in those special cases where the child is born by Caesarian section—that is through an operation that avoids the natural process of birth. In such people, something can be preserved of a truly heavenly strength—perhaps more than in those who have had to take the usual way into the world, though I have not enough biographies to prove this assumption. In the old sagas, and through the poets, something has survived that points to the fact that in olden times extraordinary deeds were expected of a person who had been "cut out" of his mother's body. Shakespeare, who had so much human wisdom, undoubtedly thought that it is a quite special destiny to be born by a "Caesarian." He would not otherwise have made this motive of such decisive importance in one of his greatest tragedies. Macbeth, who has all the dark forces on his side, still feels himself strong enough towards the end of his struggle because it was prophesized to him:

> "Be bloody, bold and resolute; and laugh to scorn
> The power of man, for none of woman born
> Shall harm Macbeth."

35

So he continues to fight furiously until he is confronted by a man who shows in his purity of character even more strength than himself. This man becomes the opponent of the powers of Hell. When, before the duel, Macduff faces his enemy, Macbeth boasts:

> "Let fall thy blade on vulnerable crests.
> I bear a charmed life, which must not yield
> To one of woman born."

To this Macduff's answer is:

> "Despair thy charm;
> And let the angel whom thou still hast serv'd
> Tell thee, Macduff was from his mother's womb
> Untimely ripp'd."

II

A birth by the use of forceps may have just the opposite effect on the child to that of a Caesarian section. In the normal course of a confinement, the head slowly presses forward and becomes gradually modelled to the maternal organism. Through the use of forceps, a sudden and powerful action takes place. The child's head is firmly seized and is subjected from outside to the pressure of the instrument. All this happens in a matter of minutes. The child is therefore far too suddenly exposed to the physical forces. As a result of this operation, children suffer from shock, and have to be treated for some time before they are able to breathe. Many backward children owe their abnormalities to an injury of the brain resulting from the use of a forceps. In these cases it is possible to see directly how the destiny of a child is changed merely by an operation badly performed.

III

One cannot be too much aware of the enormous differences for the child in the conditions before birth and after it. The great change after birth in the immediate surroundings demands that one should approach the little being only with the utmost gentleness and tenderness. At first everything, which too violently assails the sense organs, must be avoided.

A new-born child can be pictured in the following way. The little body, with its over-developed head—(the younger the child, the bigger, in proportion to the rest of the body, is the head)—this little body is surrounded by the invisible soul and spirit. As the child grows, these latter are to find their way, step by step, to physical expression. The soul must gradually enter the body. Those around the child, then, should take care that nothing is overhastened, nothing done by force, but all through real love. A mother with a true natural understanding should provide the best possible environment, and it is for this reason that her continued presence is so desirable. It would be ideal if special beds in which there was also room for the child could be made for confinements; in which a kind of "nest" could be arranged that the mother could easily reach. One could even consider building some sort of little cradle into the big bed. But if none of these alternatives is a possibility, the cradle or Moses basket should be placed as near as possible to the mother. She should always be able to listen to the delicate breathing of the baby.

How is it possible to guard against strong stimulation of the sense organs in the earliest years? I would particularly draw attention to the fact that one should avoid exposing the child to the action of soap and water. Dr. Wilhelm zur Linden has pointed out that the skin of the newborn baby is covered with a greasy substance (*vermix caseosa*), one of whose functions is that of nourishment. If this grease is removed from the skin, the baby is deprived of an important food stuff that can be of great help in the first days; without this natural covering the skin is more exposed to the external influences of heat and cold. The best course is, after birth, to clean the child only in the places where it is necessary, with a little warm oil. This should be wiped off gently in such a way that the original grease remains.

The room where the child lives must be warm, since it has been kept all the time at an even warmth in the mother's body. Next to its skin, it should have a soft vest knitted of pure wool, and the head also should be covered with a little woolen bonnet. This head covering is important during the first months in order to prevent the loss of warmth from the child, which should be avoided as much as possible. Just as the rest of the body would quickly become cold if it were not covered, so is this true also of the head in the early months. If one touches a little child's head one can immediately feel how much warmer it is than in later life. So the head should be kept covered for some time, and especially should the fontanelles be protected so that warmth shall not be lost through these openings in the skull-bones. We should always keep in mind that a child needs warmth in order to prosper. For its body it must have warmth through heating, clothing and feeding, and for its soul, warmth through the love of those who are near to it. The child has had no connection with the external world before birth—but after birth that world penetrates into it with every breath and every sense perception.

IV

We often forget that the newborn baby has hitherto lived, in its mother's womb, isolated from the world of sounds. Even though little children do not always respond to noises in their surroundings, this is anything but a proof that noise has no influence on them. The radio should never be turned on even in the nursery of a maternity home, where all the babies are put together in a row. Once when I tried to speak tactfully about this regrettable practice to a matron, I was only rewarded with a shrug of the shoulders and a contemptuous glance.

An ordinary way of speaking, not exaggerated in strength, and also the soft singing of the mother seem to be the most natural and suitable sounds for the child. These are desirable conditions that can easily be achieved at home but not in hospital.

At the beginning of its earthly life, the child's eyes should be protected from the impact of too bright a light. Rudolf Steiner recommended hanging a delicate light blue veil round the cradle; this surrounds the baby with a soft coloured light. The mother may, of course, choose a different colour if she knows exactly what is right for her own boy or girl.

I sincerely hope that in these days, when the danger of an eye infection through gonorrhea has almost disappeared, drops of the famous silver nitrate will no longer be put into babies' eyes. Thousands of children every year have had to suffer this routine practice even when there had not been the slightest danger of infection. Some of them had swollen eyes and conjunctivitis for days through chemical irritation. As far as I could discover, it was still required by law in Germany in 1951 to give the drops after birth.

V

As mentioned above, the child who is not deprived by an immediate bath or general wash of the greasy substance of the skin, has one great advantage. It receives, from the beginning, a kind of natural food-stuff, since the grease is reabsorbed, and disappears by itself in a few days.

The baby should be given the breast pretty soon after birth. This is good for both mother and child. The milk comes more easily, and the child gets enough liquid and therefore needs no artificial food supply. The first liquid from the breast, which comes before milk secretion starts, has moreover twice to three times the vitamin A content of the real milk.

There can be no doubt that the mother's milk as a rule gives the best nourishment for the infant. I shall quote a few facts to show that it will make a great difference to the child whether it is fed by the mother or artificially. A given quantity of milk from the breast contains half as much calcium as the same quantity of cow's milk. Thus, the child fed on cow's milk retains more calcium in its body than the child who is naturally fed. Whether it is richer or poorer in calcium has a great influence on the whole organism. It has been proved, for instance, that babies brought up on cow's milk have about 25% more muscle-substance than those fed on their mother's milk. Such facts, which have appeared in recent books on nutrition, show clearly that a man's whole life must be affected according to whether he has been fed in one or the other way. Modern scientists all agree that in spite of our considerable knowledge of the chemistry of metabolism, the mother's milk remains the ideal food for the baby however exactly and cleverly an artificial food may be prepared.

It is also a fact that the mother who will not or cannot feed her baby, deprives herself as well as the child of an intimate connection that is certainly maintained by breast-feeding. The giving of her milk by the mother provides the last real physical link between mother and child after birth.

Dr. zur Linden indicates that in all probability those children in whom the greasy substance of the skin has not been destroyed, and those who have not had to suffer too great a loss of heat, are less prone to the jaundice of the newly born (*Icterus neonatorum*).

The baby should be given the breast every three hours. Some mothers are frightened, at first, of nursing their babies. This must be avoided as nervousness or anxiety in the mother will make its influence felt on the child. It is not necessary to keep too strictly to the three hour intervals. Often babies will want to regulate their hours of feeding in their own way. To a certain extent such mobility in the rhythm, may be allowed; at first, and even for some time, babies often feed while still asleep.

Babies should be fed on their mother's milk until they are six months old. If they are weaned later than this, they remain too much connected with the maternal forces of inheritance and become over-dependent upon these forces. We can readily understand this statement made by Rudolf Steiner. At the end of its first half-year, the child is already trying to sit up. In this striving, as will be more fully explained later, those forces of uprightness show themselves that are working in the baby.

They are a sign of how the individuality is taking possession of the physical body. At six months, the child may reach such a stage of development that it can to a certain extent free itself from the forces of inheritance. This freedom is most easily achieved in the domain of nutrition. At half a year the child is able to digest substances other than the mother's milk without any difficulty. Besides this, observation teaches us that the child who remains too long at the breast comes to resemble its parent closely. In the past, when people loved to see in a child the image of its mother, children were still given the breast, even when they could already run about. Among peasants and gypsies this was the usual thing—and may still be.

VI

The problem of artificial feeding arises and becomes important where it is not possible to give the infant its mother's milk. Nowadays many young mothers unfortunately have not the slightest desire to feed their children themselves. It is not always the lack of milk that leads to weaning. For some time now, the reason popularly given has been an economic one; the mother either wanted to or had to go to work. Although there is some basis for this, it must also be said that women so often hear how much easier it is to handle a bottle that they are only too readily persuaded to change from breast-feeding to artificial feeding.

The question is, which is the best substitute for breast-milk? The less the food-stuff is handled, the better it will be. Fresh cow's milk, proportionally diluted, can well be recommended. The giving of dried, powdered milk is not to be thought of. It is deplorable that in some countries the great majority of artificially fed babies are given dried milk. Since it is often subsidized by the State, this form is advocated as the best. As a result of the machine-process through which it is put, dried milk is always clean, and from the chemical point of view it has the same value, but it is undoubtedly far from having the living, strengthening quality of a fresh milk. An attempt is made to counterbalance this deficiency by the artificial addition of vitamins. In our daily medical practice we see only too clearly the results of giving this much-advertised food. The rich, dried milk causes over-feeding, and one sees a lot of babies who are too fat. Many sisters and nurses in the baby clinics are inclined to show undue approval of big gains in weight, and so the young mothers feel encouraged to give their babies as much of the dried milk as possible.

The milk from the cow should be fresh. This is the best thing for babies who are deprived of their mother's milk. The animals must be healthy, and they also should be fed in a natural way. It is harmful for the animals, and consequently also for the babies, if their pastures are artificially manured, or if artificial substances are added to their feeds.

It may perhaps be of interest to know that Rudolf Steiner recommended donkey's milk for babies who are not breast-fed. Without going into the reasons for this suggestion, I want to quote a writer who—obviously not influenced by Steiner—tells of a remarkable experience. Katherine Everett* speaks in her memoirs of her own little son. He was very weak, and looked like a newly-hatched pigeon, thrown out of the nest. At three months, his weight was not much more than at birth. His mother could not feed him herself, and a French wet-nurse was

* *Bricks and Flowers*, The Reprint Society, London, 1951.

called in, but proved a failure. In desperation, the mother wrote to a friend in Ireland who recommended donkey's milk. This worked like a miracle from the first. The milk came from London, and was charged at six shillings a bottle. It was known as "Ba's champagne," and the mother was willing to do anything to get it. The child gained rapidly in weight, and became peaceful and well-developed. Later, the mother decided that it would be better to have a donkey, and she had every success in bringing up her child on that animal's milk.

VII

With babies, the importance of avoiding all forceful action cannot be stressed enough and so one must warn against the habit of holding them on the pot long before they are able to sit up alone. The idea is, of course, to get them to be clean as soon as possible. If it is done as in this country—where one might almost say that the nurse appears with the pot immediately after birth—then the effect is to induce a certain degree of consciousness in the organs of excretion. This can cause a disturbance in the life-forces of the child. It is possible, also, that this is one of the reasons why so many children suffer much later from enuresis (bed-wetting). One should never try to use a pot before the child is able to sit freely and without effort. It is about this time that children begin to understand the situation. Some medical writers speak of the age between ten and twelve months as the time when the nervous system has so matured that it is possible voluntarily to control the emptying bladder and rectum. Myrtle B. McGraw has experimented with pairs of twins. She gives the following facts. One twin was started with the pot from the third week, and his brother when he was 430 days old. The first was little more successful in using it than the second. One cannot be emphatic enough in pointing out how unnecessary, damaging, and indeed torturing it is for an infant to be forced into a function for which his organs are not yet ready. This book,* which deals with the maturing of the child's muscles and nerves, is no more than a confirmation of the facts observed in practice. For we find that healthy children who have not been bothered with the pot before 10–12 months, easily learn to be clean after that age. At about 2 years they are usually clean, if one lets them sit on the pot as soon as they ask for it.

One must always remember that the natural position for a small baby is the horizontal one. Mothers should be strongly advised always to carry their babies in the horizontal position, until they are able to sit without support.

The peaceful process of growth in the child undergoes a considerable change as the soul draws gradually into the body from birth onwards. This entry of the soul is accomplished upon a threefold path. Only two of the three gateways through which the soul is led into the body are open to our influence, namely, the way of nutrition, and the way of the sense organs. The first is opened immediately after birth; it is that of the breathing and circulation, and is beyond our control. The breathing in of air forms the radical turning point between continuous sleep during embryonic life and the awakening of consciousness.

From the moment breathing starts, the baby can already give signs of its feeling life; it cries, and thereby indicates that the

* *The Neuromuscular Maturation of the Human Infant*, Myrtle B. McGraw, Columbia University Press.

45

soul experiences with pain its entrance into its physical home. An important psysiological change takes place with the first breath, which has always been considered as the moment of animation. The blood now flows along another route, and the pulmonary circulation, which makes breathing possible, is established. The breathing rhythm in man is subject to great irregularities, especially during the first three years. These oscillations depend, on the one hand, upon the condition of the baby in the course of a given day, upon whether it is awake or asleep, attentive or dreamy, whether or not it has just had a meal, whether it feels well or unwell in itself. On the other hand, the irregularities depend upon the age of the child. The younger it is, the more is its respiration inclined to be irregular. The rate is 40–50 per minute in the newly-born, and about 24 in a two year old. At five years it is 20, and at 9 years reaches 18, the adult rate. The rhythm of breathing gives a picture of how the soul gradually models the body. Whereas the blood carries dissolved substances to all parts of the body, and with them, warmth, the breathing always causes a certain cooling down of the organism.

When, for example, long and violent muscular work results in overheating of the body, the temperature will be regulated and reduced by the breathing. (Other factors also play into this regulating process as, for instance, perspiration.) We can imagine how the breathing with its cooling effect brings about a fine and delicate forming of the organism. It is as if the building forces were called in through the breathing process. The cooling effect then plays its part here just as, in a salt solution, the influence of cold will bring about crystallization. This happens in a subtle way in the living body, and the analogy should serve only as a help in picturing the connection between the process of breathing and the shaping and forming of the child's organs. Thus we have one gateway of the soul into the physical body where the two rhythmic streams work together: the warmth-giving and dissolving bloodstream, the special significance of which is visible in the pulsating heart; and the stream of breathing that brings with the air a cooling and form-giving influence into the human being, and which finds immediate expression in the continuously expanding and contracting wall of the thorax.

Secondly, the incarnating soul follows the path along which the food is carried through the organs of metabolism.

The third road for the soul's entrance into the body is provided by the sense organs. These are directed outwards to the external world, and the nerves connected with them lead to the central nervous system.

4

THE GATEWAY OF THE WILL

I

The concept of the threefold organisation of the human being, which was taught by Rudolf Steiner, emerges quite naturally from the consideration of these three gates through which the soul of man enters the body of the child.

Nutrition has its center in the organs of metabolism. From these parts of the body, mainly, that is, from the alimentary tract with its important glands, most of the substances are provided that build up the body. Throughout life, the activity of the metabolic system penetrates into the whole organism, but it works most intensively in early childhood. This is shown by the facts. A healthy baby has usually doubled its birth weight in five months and trebled it in twelve. But only by the end of the second year is the weight four times as much as at birth.

In later life one can never see the individual so clearly given up to the enjoyment of taking in food as he is in childhood. When the baby feeds, its great activity can be seen to penetrate even into movements of the limbs. The very toes are active, and

48

sometimes the big toe even reflects the rhythm of the sucking. In this period of life, then, the connection between the metabolism and the limbs can be specially well observed. Thus Rudolf Steiner spoke of the "metabolic-limb system" as a unity. Another fact reveals itself in the feeding infant—the connection that exists between the metabolism and the will. When the child feels hungry, the will brings about a contraction in almost all the muscles, beginning with those round the mouth, and continuing down into the fingers and toes.

From the first feeding of the infant, one can clearly follow how the will penetrates into the body and lives in the limbs and the organs of metabolism. An enormous drive of will is necessary—as I shall show later—to transform the baby from the unconscious, sleeping being it is at birth, to the awake and upright human child. It is just these movements of the will accompanying the assimilation of food that make the infant into a real earthly being. The same strong will has brought the child from a spiritual existence into an earthly one. (Spiritual realities shine through some old customs, and an old Germanic practice becomes thus understandable. A child shown to the father after birth, if it had not first had any kind of food, could legally be killed if the father was not willing to accept it. But if the child had already taken so much as a drop of milk, the father had no longer the right to kill it. The child was still considered a heavenly being if no earthly nourishment had entered its body.)

II

This connection between the development of the human will, the "metabolic-limb system" and the food stream that penetrates into the organism, shows the importance of the food that is given in the early years of childhood. Much will depend upon the substances chosen and their quality. Nothing should be given to a baby that it cannot fully digest; this may endanger the whole life of the will. One example, which we owe to Rudolf Steiner, may be cited. He suggests that eggs should not be given to children until they are three; through eating eggs in the first years, man can lose that natural instinct that he should have in later years for what is the right kind of food for him.

An egg bears within it certain essential qualities. As well as its content of fairly concentrated protein, there are also present in it living forces that have the power to form completely a new being—that is, the chicken. In a way, it is asking too much of the child's digestion for it to overcome both kinds of forces. For it must be remembered that within the human body, the specific individual quality inherent in every foodstuff has to be destroyed in the ordinary course of digestion. Thus the protein of milk, for example, must shed its "cow-quality" before it can be used by the child. Any kind of food-stuff that is not broken down in the right way may cause damage. In the case of the egg, the bad effect sometimes shows itself very quickly. Children—and even adults—can become so sensitive to this substance that they develop nettlerash or asthma immediately after they have eaten eggs. (I remember a man who had an attack of asthma if he ate cake that had even a trace of egg in it.)

This reaction of people who are allergic to eggs is well-known. We will not go into the question of "allergy" here, but one can well imagine that small children (and the younger they are, the more harmful it will be) even if they are not "allergic" in the usual sense, may not be able fully to digest the egg. The result will be that something inherent in the finer processes of metabolism is harmed. Such disturbances bring about the loss of the natural instinct for the right food and the right quantity of it, first in the child, and also later when it is grown up. Quite different conditions prevail in the realm of the animals. The animal—if it is not spoiled by domestication—knows what it should eat, and how much. It is wonderful how grazing cows, horses, sheep and donkeys know what is beneficial to them. Man, too, has a natural instinct for food, although in him it is not so well-developed as in animals. But through wrong feeding, as, for instance, by eating too many eggs in early life, this instinct is lost. Is it not one of the illnesses of our times that people usually do not know what to eat or when to stop? The lack of this instinct may be considered to be one of the reasons why "indigestion" is such a frequent complaint. The cause often goes back to wrong feeding in early childhood.

Little children know when they have had enough, unless their instincts have already been spoiled. The mother or nurse must be observant in order to find out why a child will refuse food. It may be too tired, or may want to play, or perhaps its mind is occupied with something else, and it has not even noticed the dish, but often it happens also that the baby just knows it has had enough, or feels a special aversion for certain kinds of food. To force the child will only have a bad effect in later life; it will not know when it has had enough, or what food is harmful to it. Watch a child between the ages of one and two who has the right instinct for food. You will see that if it is given some fruit of which it is especially fond, for instance, the little boy or girl will eat until satisfied and then throw away the rest with the greatest unconcern. A stupid nurse or mother will be shocked,

51

and will scold the child and tell it to finish everything up instead of understanding that here is a healthy child with a healthy instinct for food.

III

The child itself shows us clearly that it is a being full of will forces—a fact to which Rudolf Steiner has specially drawn our attention. We have only to observe how an infant screams for its food. It shouts and cries when it is hungry until it gets what it wants. The element of will works powerfully upon the milk that flows into the body, so that when the milk is swallowed the way is opened for the will. The metabolic organs, being the vehicles of the will, can then become harmonized in the right way. The cry of hunger in a little child is the expression of the longing of its will to find the right way into the body. To be hungry and not to be satisfied is for the baby a true pain of the soul; it suffers because entrance is denied to the will forces.

The child who cries vigorously for food, summons the will into its body by the effort of crying. Thus, a remark of Rudolf Steiner may become understandable. He said that a child who screams and cries powerfully in its early years, can develop strong moral forces in later life. In other words, the child reveals in the strength of its cries the latent power of a will that is longing for incarnation. Now, whence does all true moral force originate? Surely from a rightly guided will. So a child who cries with all its might shows that it is trying to lead the will into its organism. In this way it will be able to build a strong body, with whose help man can gain the inner power of morality. Thus we see that the powers of will gradually enter into the body and take hold of the organs. Having gained such strong organs, man is later able to bring true creativeness into the world around him. It is obvious, therefore, if we consider the development of a human being in this way, that for the later years of man, a lot depends upon the guidance given in childhood.

IV

One of the greatest efforts the human being has to make in his development lies in that activity of the will that brings the child into the erect posture. At present, a danger exists in the wish to speed up the early development without considering the consequences for later years. The child should but slowly bring its will into action; it then creates a well-prepared ground for soul and mind. At the beginning of the century there was a disease in young children of which people were afraid. This was rickets. It is a condition in which growth is delayed. The children who suffer from it become too weak to bring their will into full play. The baby can no longer lift its head, which then becomes too heavy, while the bones of the skull soften. Later, sitting up is delayed, because the spine and ribs are not sufficiently firm. Finally, it cannot walk at the right time because the limb bones have lost the strength that is necessary for the upright posture. Nowadays, rickets has become less common. Only a few cases occur in civilized countries, and most doctors laugh at the danger. They have learnt how to prevent it by means of sunlight, fresh air and those foods that contain the forces of light—known by the general and abstract name of Vitamin D. But strangely enough, children are still given cod liver oil, which is supposed to prevent rickets. This is something completely paradoxical; a preventive treatment is undertaken against a disease that has naturally disappeared under modern hygienic conditions. A "successful" struggle is fought against an enemy that is almost non-existent. (Needless to say, rickets occurs under bad hygienic conditions, and then it has to be treated.)

We may consider this as a symbol of what, in general, people are aiming to achieve. Whereas before, the mistake was made of slowing down the development of the child's will, today nearly all educational and hygienic measures tend to speed up the child's development as much as possible. Everything is done to force the individual quickly into its body.

The child shows the power of its personality and its specifically human qualities when it tries to become upright, and each child must be allowed to reach this stage in its own time.

The child needs, as its inmost support, a well-built skeleton. The process of acquiring the erect posture takes place in three phases. They correspond to the three systems of the organism. First, the child tries to lift its head, and one should not fall into the temptation of helping it. It will start by itself as soon as the bones of the head have attained the necessary firmness, and all support from outside is harmful. We have only to lay the child on its tummy if we want to find out how far it can turn and lift its head.

After a few months, the next step follows. The child makes an effort to sit up. Again, one must not make it sit up before it can do so through its own strength. Unfortunately, babies are often made to sit supported by two pillows, and thus forced too soon into the upright position. A baby put into this position is a picture of misery to anyone who has a natural feeling for it. It looks like an empty sack that has been propped up. It does not fall down again, because it is artificially supported, but the soul is not able to penetrate into the little body and so the baby looks more like a lifeless marionette. The look in its eyes, which are living mirrors of the soul, becomes vacant and helpless.

In the natural course of growth, the child tries to bring the middle part of its body into the upright position as soon as it can lift its head. We should remember how much strength is needed in all the little vertebrae and ribs and the appropriate muscles in order to bring the child into a sitting position; arms and hands have to help, and we must not forget that the little round head has also to be kept straight!

The third phase is standing and walking. This calls for a real firmness of legs and feet, which must now be penetrated by the will. The time for this third phase does not come until the first and second are already achieved.

Thus we see that a threefold impulse of will is necessary to change the child's position from the horizontal to the vertical. Careful observation also reveals a remarkable fact—namely that another process of development takes place at the same time that is equally essential to the achievement of the upright posture in the child. This is connected with the impulse to move forwards. Strangely enough, here also three different phases succeed one another, but this time in the opposite order to that of lifting the head, sitting and walking. First, the child tries to push it's whole body forward. To begin with, this is only possible when it lies on its tummy and attempts to slide forward with the help of its limbs. Thus a kind of creeping movement is developed, the hands and feet sliding and pushing against whatever is underneath. Little headway is made with this creeping until the child is able to sit up.

The second phase usually occurs after a few months, when the child rises onto its knees, and is supported by arms and hands resting on the ground. Children love to crawl "on all fours," though the expression is not quite correct. Some babies can get along fast in this position, and are for a long time loath to give it up.

The third phase of forward movement, which does not last long, also has its own peculiar gait. The child no longer supports itself on its knees; instead, the legs are stretched out and stiffened at the knee-joint, and the hind-end raised up. The arms are also stretched out straight, and the child now really does walk on its hands and feet. It no longer crawls, but truly walks "on four legs." After this, it can usually pretty soon walk upright. It is a mistake to suppose that the upright position is brought about by a single impulse of will, developing from the head gradually down towards the feet—that is, in the direction in which the skeleton develops. In reality, there is a second impulse of will that works in just the opposite direction from the feet upwards towards the head. This second drive has its point of attack rather in the muscular system (though the skeleton also participates in it), while the first-mentioned stream of the will is connected more with the bones and their formation.

Some understanding of the riddle of walking is to be found in the harmonious working together of the two currents of the will.

V

In these days, it is becoming more and more usual to submit everything to external necessity. This procedure has now encroached even upon the method of bringing up children. Many mothers find it difficult to cope with the constantly active small child who is just beginning to walk and find its way about, and at the same time to look after their husbands and houses. The usual thing, then, is to take the children to a nursery school where nurses from welfare institutions can have the care of them during the day.

But children still have to be looked after from the end of the first year until they are old enough to go to a nursery school. Now what do mothers do with these little beings who crawl about, try to stand, and want to run all over the place? They are put into play-pens. This has become a matter of course almost all over the world, and it hardly ever occurs to anyone to think what it means to the child. Just try for once, without prejudice, to realize what this play-pen really is. Imagine that you have never seen such a thing before. Here, enclosing the child, is a square wooden construction, its sides measuring between two and three yards each; four lengths of wooden railing ending above and below in narrow transverse strips. According to the height of the child, the play-pen comes up to its chest or its shoulders. The whole thing reminds one of a square fence, or one could call it a kind of chicken-run—open above, since there is no danger that the child will flutter away. But it could also deservedly be named a portable prison; a limit is set to the movements of the young inhabitant of this earth by the four sides. It can be erected anywhere—in kitchen, sitting-room, bath-room or garden. If it is put in the garden, it will depend upon the adults whether it stands in the full glare of the sun or in the cool shade. To entertain the child, all kinds of objects are put into the little prison; there is a ball, which is usually thrown out at once, and, since it does not come back by itself, leaves its owner crying inside; a big teddy bear lies unnoticed in a corner; old and new dolls have here their meeting-place; cooking spoons and crayons are scattered about; even tin cans are apparently not considered unworthy offerings for the prisoner. Interest in these treasures soon fades—if indeed it ever existed. The child is usually to be seen leaning against the wooden bars with its arms hanging over the side. It stares at everything, follows with its eyes everything that goes on outside its prison, and tries to communicate by sounds or face movements with the beings beyond the four enclosing railings. But if it cannot make any connection with the world outside, it will often begin to shake the bars with all its might; some children do this with real fury! How pointless then seem those colored beads that are threaded on to one side of many play-pens, and whose purpose is to occupy or amuse the baby!

The grown-ups are hardly ever consciously aware of what is happening to this child who has for many hours on end to lead the life of a prisoner. But close observation will reveal quite clearly that certain hopes rise up again and again in the imprisoned being; rise up and are dispelled in the next moment. The adult lets his thoughts come and go in complete freedom, brooking no hindrance, and allowing no limits. This freedom that the adult gives to his thoughts is just what the child needs for the movements of his physical body. Each time some living thing appears outside the pen, the child longs at once to make some contact with this "outside" being. He hopes unconsciously for sympathy, love, joy and the fulfillment of his wishes from beyond the square enclosure. Nearly every time he is disappointed and feels himself rejected by the world. Just as we feel depressed if we cannot think a thought through to its conclusion, or if we are no longer allowed to consider things freely in our soul, so does the child suffer when he is restrained from moving about. One can see clearly how much, when the child is left alone, the otherwise free inhaling and exhaling of air is hampered. Such disturbances of the bodily functions lead to organic disturbances after a time. One can easily imagine the psychological consequences in later years of such a wrong treatment of children. There may then show itself an inner lack of freedom, a certain anxiety, and a tendency to become over-occupied with the inner life.

There is another unfortunate mistake made with children, to which I must draw attention. It concerns the way in which, between the ages of one and a half, and three or four, many of them are taken out walking. I mean the use of reins, as they are called, that are fastened round the chests of these children. These reins are made of leather straps, often colored green, red or brown, and decorated with flowers or little bells. Attached to each side at the back is a longer strap by means of which the adult can lead the child, like a little horse.

What is the advantage of this to the mothers, grannies and so on, who use it? It means that they do not have to pay so much attention to the child as they walk through the streets. The child, of course, runs in front and can be kept back by a slight pull on the rope, like a dog on a lead. But it can run safely, and does not have to be continually called back. Also, if the adult is

59

tall, she will not have to bend down to reach the child's hand, and her own hands are free to carry the shopping, since the strap can be wound round a finger. Her mind also is free to wander, and she can watch the people and the shops, and forget the child altogether, knowing at the same time that no harm can come to it. It will not fall or be lost, nor can it easily be run over.

All reasonable people, then, will have to admit that the invention of children's reins is a clever one that can only be considered a blessing and a great convenience.

But whoever has experienced with human understanding what it means to hold a child by the hand on a walk will realize how much the child loses (and the adult too) by being led through the streets like a little animal. The great wrong that is done to the child if he is put on a lead is that the grown-up does not treat him as an equal, but rather as if he were an animal. A four-legged creature cannot as a general rule be led in any other way. But the child, who has managed to lift himself up after crawling about for a certain time on all fours—the child has striven to become an upright man. He is able to offer his heart to the world and move his hands freely in space. If we take a child by the hand, we can feel how all his inner warmth streams towards us in confidence. Through this contact of hands, we can ourselves experience everything that moves the child as we walk with him through the streets. The pressure of his little fingers reveal his joy and pain, curiosity and shyness, love and aversion. It is as if the two hands (the child's and the adult's) were carrying on an intimate conversation. This gives to the little boy or girl a feeling of protection and complete confidence; while to the grown-up it gives a sense of holy responsibility. Older children seem sometimes to realize the importance of being allowed to guide a younger brother or sister by the hand.

But leading reins separate man from man, the growing from the grown. This may seem to be something unimportant and of little consequence, but it nevertheless points to a great social problem of our time: how are people to find their way to one another?

For the sake of completeness, a third wrong practice will be mentioned, this also having to do with a way of taking little children about.

In these days we often see a little boy or girl, sometimes not more than two or three years old, sitting on a kind of basket-seat attached behind the saddle of a bicycle. Closer observation usually reveals that the little passenger is not getting much pleasure out of this kind of journey through the world. The adult has to give all his attention to the road and is hardly aware of the child, who therefore feels lonely on his little seat. If he wants to look forward, he is confronted by the large back of his father or mother, so that he must feel rather like someone who has to sit so near to a wall that the bricks are almost touching his chin. He can move little, except to turn his head to right or left, and this some children do all the time in their desire to see more than just the parental back. If it is a stormy day, the wind blowing in their faces must be a real torture to them; one can see them sometimes gripping their flying hair with both hands and blinking their eyes. If a child in such a position wants to say anything, no one can hear him. The parent remains unaware of his desire, and apparently unconcerned. So the child is driven into a feeling of isolation and loneliness. He is bereft of that protection he needs so much, especially in those early years.

VI

It has been mentioned before that uprightness can be achieved only if the main support of the body, the bony system, is built up in the right way. The metabolism of man so functions that the important substances, calcium and phosphorus, are distributed in the correct amounts in the blood. They are then used as needed to form the skeleton. One cannot imagine with what delicacy this work is carried out; how one spicule of bone after another rises up, and is broken down, only to be re-erected and strengthened. Into all these processes the human will penetrates, gradually shaping the body of the individual.

A full understanding of this delicate working at once makes it clear that on no account must there be any interference with the child's formation of its organism. Anything tending to speed it up must be avoided, unless essential for reasons of health. Unfortunately, every effort is being made at present just in the direction of speeding up the whole development of the child, starting even during the embryonic life. Although the discovery of the substances known as vitamins was a wonderful one, their use as an anti-rachitic prophylaxis has a devastating effect. The well-known vitamin D—nowadays already a veteran among vitamins—has a particular influence on the calcium and phosphorus content of the blood. Vitamin D is stored especially in the liver, but also to a certain extent in the skin, spleen, brain and bones. The stored vitamin is slowly released from these organs and causes a certain retention of phosphorous and calcium in the body. As shown before, the mother's milk contains all those substances in a truly wonderful way in the best balanced proportions necessary for the baby's food. American food specialists have found that both mother's and cow's milk contain, to every 2 pints, about 30–40 units of vitamin D.

In their opinion this is far too little, and the cow's milk, at least, must be made richer in vitamin D. Dried milk, which is used so much in the feeding of infants, is accordingly "strength-ened" in America with 400 units—ten times as much as there is in the natural cow's and mother's milk. This means that the artificially fed baby gets—in America at least—much more vitamin D from its milk than does the breast-fed baby. Remember besides this that every teaspoonful of cod liver oil contains 600–900 units of vitamin D. Every mother who goes to a children's welfare center in England is recommended to give her child cod liver oil. Since she gets it free, it is obvious that all children are overdosed with vitamin D whether they need it or not. What does this mean? That the infant is quite arbitrarily given a substance that causes a higher retention of phosphorus and calcium in the body so that already at this tender age the skeleton is built up, quite without relation to individual need. The bones are made stronger and more solid than they would naturally be, and this indicates that they are not so delicately formed. We have seen that it is possible to prove that babies who are given more than the minimum amount of vitamin D grow to more than average weight and size. But this must have its definite repercussions on the whole organism, which will certainly become denser, and so correspondingly less permeable to soul and spirit—a less responsive instrument. Of course there is the great advantage that hardly any children suffer from rickets, and they also learn more quickly to stand and to walk. But it is rarely taken into consideration how much more quickly these children become sclerotic and prematurely old. They will not necessarily die earlier, and may live a long life, but in their whole being they will be stiff, and it will be hard to overcome their earthly heaviness.

To prevent misunderstanding by those who have little training in biological thinking, I must stress that it is not the calcium retained in the infant body that will become sedimented in the blood vessels of the old man—but rather that through the quickened development at such an early age many of the organs lose much of their vitality. The organism grows coarser and this leads toward the end of life to the speeding up of the process of growing old. One could easily argue against such statements that no real proof has been given of their validity. But is it necessary to wait until the unfortunate results are shown? If unbiased thinking can understand these ideas, why not alter the relevant methods of medical practice? It was Rudolf Steiner who long ago pointed out that forcing a child to stand and walk would lead to premature sclerosis and rheumatism in the later years of life. Now, from the evidence of all kinds of modern experiments, we can understand such an assertion perhaps better than was possible thirty years ago.

This tendency to speed up the development of children is to be seen also in the introduction of physical exercises for babies, now being advocated more than ever before. An unnatural development of the functions of the limbs is the result. This exercising of the baby, which is spoken of in such glowing terms, is just the opposite of what should be done. It is not only damaging to the health of the baby, but one ought not even to allow a young child to move its arms and legs about too freely. It should really be kept undisturbed, surrounded by the warmth of love, in a calm and peaceful atmosphere. Then only will the organs be formed in the right way. If one does not take these requirements of the infant seriously into account, there will be certain definite consequences. The first ten months are important in this respect. The child who does not grow up in the atmosphere it needs will suffer in later years when its soul will no longer have the right connection with the body.

The soul will then strive too much towards the periphery and become as unstable as the limbs were fidgety in the early years. Restlessness and superficiality will develop. One way of preventing this condition is by wrapping the baby firmly up in a shawl, especially at night. A right balance must be struck so that the child is not too much hindered in the movements of its limbs. In practice, it is perhaps advisable, until the fifth month, to wrap the baby up firmly at night and more loosely during the day. It is likely to become too heavy, lose its inner mobility and be hampered in its speech if it is kept wrapped up for too long a period. Congestion may also arise, resulting in asthma or stammering.

The child begins to move as soon as the will can enter the body, and it will then practice movements of its own accord. It will go on trying to lift its head until it is tired and then stop. For the baby knows best of itself when it has done enough, and nobody should interfere from outside and invent special exercises for strengthening the spine or muscles. It has become a bad habit in our times not to differentiate enough between a baby, a schoolboy of 14, and an adult. The conclusion is drawn that what is healthy for an adult and a youth—let us say gymnastic exercises—will also be healthy for a small child. From such reasoning the idea of hardening came about, and is highly thought of in connection with the bringing up of children. But cold baths or sponges for babies are quite wrong; nor should they be exposed to cold air without being well protected against all loss of warmth. These cold shocks have the effect of driving the consciousness too intensively into the body. The danger arises that the children will suffer a kind of stiffening of their organs, which will lead to illnesses through lack of resistance in the body. The resistance of the organism, as it is called, is in reality nothing but a sign of its great inner vitality, and it is just here, in its inner vitality, that the damage is done through toughening the body by subjecting it to gymnastics and cold water.

How many colds could be avoided—both in the early years, and probably also in later life—if children were only kept warm enough during at least the first seven years. This warmth is needed by the growing child if it is to build up its body in the right way. Then it will have the power of resistance later on. Only notice how many small children have cold hands and feet in autumn and winter! They are not protected enough. How cold, too, are the bedrooms in this country! Everyone in the British Isles moans and groans because he "catches one cold after another." Millions are spent on the lost hours of work of insured people, and on cough mixtures in the bad times of the year. Experiments have been made on living human beings in the last few years, with a view to finding out more about the "common cold." Cod liver oil, vitamins and vaccines are provided to fight against this evil. But hardly anybody has suggested starting with the children. They do not need armies of chemists, but they should be warmly clothed, live in warm rooms, and be fed in a reasonable way.

The cutting of the first teeth is also a manifestation of the will. It is connected with those forces that bring about the upright posture. There is usually a correspondence between the time of getting the first teeth and the time of becoming upright. One finds that those children who walk early get their first teeth early. A great effort of the will working in the organism is needed to make that hardest substance in man, which is in the teeth, grow into the upward and downward direction. Modern scientists and doctors often smile at the mention of the difficulties that are said to exist at the time of the first dentition. Yet most practitioners and mothers are convinced that the time of the cutting of teeth is a critical one for children. They are moody, unwilling to eat, restless, and have disturbed nights. There is a tendency also to intestinal troubles and temperatures. The cutting of teeth concentrates all strength in one direction and weakens the other parts of the body. The effort of the striving will can become so great that cramps are caused. This is understandable if we watch the strong will of a child as it is manifested a little later. Such observation gives us an insight into the strength of the organic revolution at the time of teething. The will of the child between one and two can become quite unmanageable. Suppose it wants to go through a door. It will try with all its might to attain its objective. If the obstacle is too great—the intervention of an adult, perhaps—then some children become furious, and throw themselves on the ground and scream. The forces that are manifested outwardly in such a fit of rage are those that earlier were working inwardly as organic forces. The will works hard in cutting the teeth; if the work is too difficult, then the whole body becomes involved in the struggle; it is as if the will became blind with rage! It exerts the same degree of strength inwardly on the organs at the time of teething as it displays outwardly later, when some obstacle stands in its way. The congestion resulting from a will that finds no outlet may lead to the convulsions of dentition. Muscular spasms and convulsions are nothing but the outcome of an uncontrolled life of the will in those organs that should be its instruments—in this case the muscles.

Certain cramps may be mentioned in this connection because they can be understood in the same way as the convulsions of dentition. I mean those cramps of early childhood in which there are convulsions of the whole body and limbs. The child loses consciousness and the fits may become dangerous, especially if they last too long. The cause often lies in wrong feeding, as in the case of rickets. There is usually a calcium deficiency in the blood of the little patients.

What does this mean? The will nature of the human being is striving to establish itself rightly in the body. But through the lack of certain substances it is no longer able to penetrate the organism in a regular and harmonious way. However this situation may have arisen, whether by organic weakness or by some glandular disturbance, the congestion of will leads to the above-mentioned fits.

Will activity is always connected with an increase of warmth. The working muscle has a greater blood supply and is warmer than the resting one. So we have to imagine the fits as corresponding to an inner congestion of warmth. Thus we find fever and swollen gums as the signs of inflammatory condition during teething. The cramps follow if there is no outlet for the will. For this reason, brushing of the skin and the use of an irritant such as mustard in a hot bath are the best treatment when such a fit occurs. In this way one can achieve a diversion of warmth to the skin. The periphery is heated, and the central congestion is relieved. In difficult cases it may be necessary to give some kind of narcotic that can to a certain extent paralyze the warmth organization of the body, and thus drive the will out of the affected organs by force. The convulsions will stop and the right regulation of warmth will establish itself again.

VIII

One can hardly discuss the welfare of the child during the first years of life without entering into the question of vaccination. The present view is that all children should be vaccinated for smallpox between the ages of three and six months. Most of them are also inoculated against diphtheria and whooping cough before the completion of their first year. To these we must add the possibility of inoculation against tuberculosis. This is practiced in some countries, and emanates mainly from France. In some countries, tuberculosis inoculation is only performed where there is a danger to the children resulting from their environment. I do not intend here to discuss the pros and cons of immunization and vaccination. I only wish to describe what happens to a child who has to undergo such prophylactic treatment. Take, for example, a baby of six months who has been vaccinated against smallpox. The child has been working on the gradual building up of its physical body through the forces of the will. Whatever food was taken into the organism has been broken down by the metabolic processes. For only when, in the process of digestion, it has lost its own specific character can any food substance remain in the organism without causing disturbance. Thus the glands of the metabolic system bring about the complete destruction of the food, and they also make it possible for the child to build up its own individual body through the working of the will organism. From this point of view, the food given to the child must be considered rather as a stimulus to excite the metabolic processes. The glands of the digestive tract gradually bring about, through their activity, those conditions necessary for the will to enter the body. It is in the warmth of the blood that the realm of the will is to be found. But this realm must be properly prepared. Only by the breaking down of all foreign substances before they reach the bloodstream can this be achieved. The proteins of the food, for example, must be so changed that they carry no trace of their original character into the blood. Now, through the power of his will, the child can form his own individual body out of his blood, which contains all the matter necessary to build up the organism. Of course, the very small child needs some time to accomplish all this. As shown before, the substance most easily digested is as a rule the mother's milk. The destruction of this milk, which is, so to speak, closely related to the child, requires the least effort, and so the yet tender forces of the child are spared. The breast fed child can easily digest the protein in its mother's milk, and the development of its metabolic system is thereby neither speeded up nor delayed. So its organs can be built up in the right way.

The vaccine lymph, as it is called, is nothing but the contents of an attenuated smallpox pustule taken from a calf. Through vaccination the vaccine, which has been formed in the animal, penetrates into the child's organism via the skin. As a result, a definite reaction occurs in the baby that may be looked upon as a strong inner drive of the will. A foreign substance has forcibly entered the body and caused it to become slightly ill. The blister that develops is an external sign of this illness. But just that activity that produces the little vesicle also brings about the formation of a kind of protective net in the blood of the vaccinated person. He or she now has for a certain number of years an immunity to smallpox. The expression "protective net" is used only as a picture to make the conception of "immunity" more understandable. It refers to a force that is implanted in the human organism by vaccination. This force is made up of two components. One originates from the animal that provides the vaccine lymph, the other is the impulse of will in the human being, who wants to overcome the intruder. From the point of view of a steady and harmonious development, both components must give rise to far-reaching disturbances in the organism.

As regards the inner impulse of will that is demanded of the child in its reaction to the vaccine lymph, this is something far in advance of what would be natural to development at this stage. Many of the diseases of childhood have their own right times of occurrence, and the reactions they call forth in the child are quite justified at these times. But the illness resulting from vaccination—if such an expression may be allowed—is quite arbitrarily brought on and forces the child to make an effort of will that is beyond it at this time.

As to the vaccine lymph itself, it is clear that something is here implanted in the body that is quite foreign to it. Since it is introduced through the blood and lymph system, it still retains its animal nature, in contrast to the ordinary food, which loses its

71

specific characteristics in its passage through the metabolic system. Thus, as a result of vaccination, a substance is introduced directly into the blood stream that does not belong to the child's own organization. It might be argued that the amount of lymph given is very small; this is no argument at all, since this small amount has yet the power to prevent so serious an illness as smallpox. Furthermore, the development of medical science has shown that very small quantities can have very powerful effects. This is borne out not only by homoeopathic medicine, but also by a study of those substances called vitamins, hormones and ferments, all of which, in small quantities, produce remarkable reactions.

While not denying the fact that vaccination does work prophylactically, one may still draw attention to the harmful effect that such a treatment has upon mankind. One can really speak of mankind in this connection, since vaccination laws exist all over the world. It must be stressed, of course, that the earlier in life the vaccination is done, the greater the consequences will be. Both the prematurely caused reaction, which indicates a physical effort of the organism, and the implanting of the "protective net" with the help of the animal power will have a weakening effect upon that which is specifically human in the child. The animals from which the lymph is taken are far more hardened and coarse in their bodies than is man. The latter takes a long time to develop from the baby to the adult, but with the animals it is quite different. They grow, as a rule, quickly and have little of that possibility of development that the human being has. Rudolf Steiner's teaching throws light on this fact; according to him, animals are beings which, in a primeval age, developed too quickly. They were not able to wait long enough before they formed a physical body, and so they now attain their adult form too quickly, becoming one-sided, stiffened and hardened as compared with man. A detailed account of this is given in Steiner's *Occult Science** and other books. It may be interesting to consider the animals as here described, and at the same time to realize that such laws of nature are still valid; the child whose growth and education are speeded up undergoes a development that bears a resemblance to the old development of animals. As described above, it becomes more quickly hardened and sclerotic in old age if one tries to hurry on the different stages of its growth.

As a result of vaccination, man loses something that is peculiar to him alone. The vaccinated child is pervaded by an animal force that makes its organs grow coarser. This reflects on the soul, which then in later years becomes more materialistic in its outlook than it would have been without the influence of the early vaccination. Such a consideration—a strange one perhaps to some people—helps one to understand why Steiner could say that there is an inner connection between the spread of materialism throughout modern civilization and vaccination against smallpox that is performed everywhere.

It seems likely that everything that I have here said about the effect of vaccination holds good for all those kinds of immunization in which matter is taken from the blood or lymph of an animal and given to man by a way that avoids the metabolic route. There is a difference with the kind of immunization in which attenuated germs or their poisonous products are used. In such cases—when the attenuated germs have not passed through

---

* *An Outline of Occult Science,* Anthroposophic Press, Spring Valley, N.Y.

a higher animal—the main danger lies in the fact that a pathological process occurs that has nothing to do with the child's natural development at the time. The importance of such a consideration is by no means merely theoretical. It has happened, for instance, that children who were immunized against diphtheria, or against diphtheria and whooping cough together, have fallen ill with poliomyelitis one month after immunization. In these cases, the injected limb (leg or arm) invariably became paralyzed. This shows that the immunization calls forth an intense reaction in the organism. The reaction may be so strong that some other quiescent illness (in the above case, poliomyelitis) is aroused. On the other hand, the many ill effects that do not show themselves until much later in life are not taken into account in these times; this is not, of course, to say that they do not exist.

IX

The will of a child reveals itself strongly during the time when it is awake and on the go. All the more reason, then, to make sure that it gets its rest. One cannot lay enough stress on the necessity for children to have long hours of rest. I have already said that small children should sleep as long as they want to, but also, from the end of the first six months until the third year, it is of the greatest importance that they should have several hours break during the day. Before the child can walk, it usually sleeps of its own accord during the day and then it should not be disturbed. It becomes more difficult when they can walk. Some mothers are ambitious to make their children walk as soon as possible. They stand them up, hold them upright, and entice them to run. I have said above that this is harmful to the child. One should always avoid forcing them. Crooked legs, weak ankles, flat feet, curvatures of the spine can be the immediate results, to say nothing of the effects that follow in later life, such as rheumatic and sclerotic diseases.

This is one wrong way of treating children—making them tired by forcing them to do something for which they are not ready.

Another way of tiring a child out, is to chase a baby about without knowing when it has had enough. One must understand how it is with such a little boy or girl. It runs, perhaps, round in a circle in the garden, or indoors round the table. Its will must be active. But on the other hand it has not the strength at this early age to put a stop to its will. An impulse takes hold of it, and the child must go on running. The understanding mother or teacher should be able to recognize such a situation and intervene in the right way. As soon as she sees that the child continues to race about or to do something repeatedly only because it cannot stop, she must find a clever way of diverting it. How this is done must be left to the moment and to what the situation demands, but it must be done gently and in accordance with the child's mood—never abruptly. The right moment is chosen, and the child quietened down.

A danger to children in the opposite direction lies in the adult's aim to be always "educating." Whatever the child tries to do, it is always suppressed. It is not allowed to go to the kitchen, to the stairs, to the garden. There is forever some precept as to what the child is or is not allowed. As a result the child becomes fidgety without getting tired in the natural way that is necessary for a good sleep.

Every child should have a rest and a sleep for one or two hours at the end of the morning, even for a long time after it has learned to walk. Then when it wakes up, it will be time for the midday meal. Some children, if they seem tired, may even need a short rest between midday and the evening.

Children who are not overtired sleep much better and more quietly at night. A little music, either sung or played on the flute or lyre after the evening prayer is a great help. It prepares the child's mind for the night. Later on, after the third year, they can have a fairy tale. The holiness that comes upon the child in sleep should already cast its shadow upon the mood that prevails before. A child will flourish if there is a regular rhythm between the will working during the day when it is awake, and the will building up the growing organism in sleep. Then the body can become that instrument for which the child was already longing before birth.

VI

THE GATEWAY OF THE SENSES

I

The will in man is activated from within, and gradually takes hold of the organs in its striving towards the periphery. The desire for food, for example, that comes from the depths of the body, goes through the muscles. It makes the child more and more restless, right into its limbs where the longing for food expresses itself. The little mouth opens wide, the jaw muscles are active, the circular muscles of the mouth contract—until at last the milk is given. Then the gateway of the senses, which leads in the opposite direction, is opened from the outside towards the center. The sense of taste demonstrates clearly how the path of the senses leads from the periphery deep into the inner part of the child's organism. The child unites itself wholly with the matter that is brought to it from outside. In this connection, one can very well see what near neighbors are the world of the will and the world of the senses in early life. If we carefully observe the feeding baby, we can discover two currents running through the tender little body. First the great wave of tension originating from the rising will that demands food; then the wave of relaxation, resulting from the joy of tasting the milk. The greater the hunger, the quicker one tension follows after another, and one relaxation after another. The baby is quiet again when its hunger is appeased.

Something quite characteristic of the senses can be learned from the process of tasting. A close contact is brought about between the milk flowing into the body and the organs of taste, and thereby the outer world is driven with great intensity into the inner world of man. In tasting, one becomes wholly open to the outer world. This is quite obvious, but the same thing happens, though in a more subtle way, in seeing and hearing. The vibrations of the air on which sound travels have their connection with the ears, light and darkness with the eyes. These things are but briefly and simply alluded to here, but one should not forget how complicated are all the details. The vibrations of the air, for instance, never in fact meet the inner part of the organ of hearing; nevertheless, certain vibrations are transferred to the inner ear. Again, it is the external world that immerses itself in man's inner organism. The same holds good in a way for the eye into which light and darkness and the colors that are derived from them enter. For a child it is a matter of the greatest importance that the external world penetrates into him through his sense organs. More will be said later on about the particular senses.

The small child, wanting to take possession of its body can only do so gradually. One could say, from the external point of view, that the outer world builds itself into man by ways of the eyes, ears and all the sense organs, but it would also be true, from the inner point of view—the point of view of man—to say that we go out through our sense organs into the world that surrounds us.

In the case of the child, this relationship with the external world is very strong. We need only look at the way in which children gaze at things. They lose themselves wholly in the perception of a man, an animal, a moving train. They open their mouths wide and drink in everything that comes from outside; at the same time their own being goes completely out into the external happenings. More than he ever does in later life, the young child becomes entirely eye or ear, or any other sense organ. Thus we can see how important for his whole life the surroundings must be in which a child grows up. On the one hand, he lives wholly and strongly outside, in the external world, and on the other, he comes back again wholly and strongly into himself.

For example, a child who sees a little dog when he is a year old, can be absolutely absorbed in the sight. Then, when he has almost swallowed the animal with his eyes, he comes back again into himself. When, so to speak, he returns to himself, the child brings to his organs all that he experienced when he saw the dog. As far as the eye is concerned, the two happenings can be distinctly separated. When the child goes out, the eyelids are widely opened; when he comes back to himself, they are quickly closed for a moment. The child, who gives himself up to his surroundings, keeps his eye-lids open for much longer than the grown-up, who is not so much lost in gazing upon what is around him, and blinks more frequently.

II

The awakening of the sense organs in an infant should be gentle and gradual. Why? Because the meeting with the outer world brings about a certain damping down of the forces of growth. This has its right place in helping to give form to the organism, but it should not be too forceful an influence in early life.

The formative processes resulting from the impact of the external world are especially active in childhood, although they do work on into old age. In some professions, for instance, one can see how certain efforts of the eyes are reflected in the character of the face. Fishermen and sailors, who direct their gaze into the far distance, have characteristic faces. This is exaggerated and may even become a caricature in a professional sportsman. Or again one can think of the texture of the skin in sailors and even farmers, which is caused by the continual exposure to wind and weather. In this case it is the skin as bearer of the sense of touch that is formed by the breezes of the atmosphere. In contrast, the blind who cannot use their eyes at all acquire features that are also characteristic; they are over-soft and expressionless. Even the skin and muscles seem to be less formed in a blind than in a seeing person.

The development of children will be guided in the right way if at an early age they are not too much exposed to the external world. It was for this reason that soft lights and colors were recommended for the baby, and soft woolen underwear and warm rooms—in short everything to counteract strong sense impressions.

The accounts given by outstanding people who could

remember their early childhood plainly show how slowly the external world acquires an outline for the small child. It is clear that a forceful penetration by the world of senses into the baby has a paralyzing effect and brings in the formative influences too early.

One does not need much advice upon how to behave with a baby if one bears the following facts in mind and acts accordingly! The forces of growth work in a child in just the same way as they work in outer nature. They are like the forces of artistic creation. This is why Rudolf Steiner repeatedly quotes Goethe's essay on "Nature." There the great artist, nature, is described with incomparable sublimity; how she builds and forms and shapes. In one place Goethe writes, "She lives in countless children, and yet the Mother—where is she? She is the accomplished artist: from the most simple materials she achieves high contrast and without seeming effort full perfection; clearest outline, yet always overlaid with softness. Each of her works has a being all its own; each one of her phenomena has the most isolated concept, and yet all are one."

For parents and teachers, these words can become a living force through which they can protect the growing child and give the right help at the right moment. It is of the greatest possible support to the forming and shaping of the child's organs if it can see and hear objects that have an inherent artistic beauty. For here, in the way it builds up the trabeculae of a vertebra, or the network of muscle fibers that form the heart, is the beauty in nature. The delicately colored veils surrounding the baby take away the hard contours from the things its eyes perceive. Only soft sounds, too, should come to its ears. There is nothing better for a baby to hear than the gentle voice of a human being, or the sound of a lyre, which, like the harp, has something in it of the beating of the waves but yet is not so powerful. For the first few months, the violin is too harsh. There are some children who cry if a violin is played in the same room. Everything that is offered to the child through the gateway of the senses should be beautiful and unobtrusive. It may then be seen or heard repeatedly. A child is never bored by the frequent repetition, for instance, of songs and verses if this is done in a reasonable way; neither, later on, does it refuse to play the same games over and over again. Just as the coming and going of the sea gradually works on the forming of the coastline, so does repetition bring the right force into the baby for the building of its body.

III

What he experiences of the outer world through his senses, is of the greatest importance for the child. The senses help him to live in that world. It is easy to understand how we expand outwards into the different qualities around us through our eyes, our ears and our sense of taste; we penetrate into the sweetness of sugar, into the blueness of the sky; we are carried away by the vibrating tones of an instrument. Furthermore, not only do we live through our sense organs in the world around us, but what we can see, hear or taste, is brought back into our organism. This going out and coming back through the sense organs is especially strong in a child. By it, the body is shaped in its finer structure. What the child receives through the refreshing sweetness of honey, the peace of a blue sky, the tenderness of a musical sound, provides a building force quite different from what comes to him from the monotonous sweetness of white sugar, the dead blue of a tasteless garment, or the shrill tone of a whistle. Thus its surroundings can be to a baby now helpful, now damaging.

Of the greatest significance is Rudolf Steiner's description of an additional series of sense organs through which we penetrate into the outer world, as well as into ourselves, in a far deeper and more delicate way. He speaks of a sense of warmth. This is important for a child. Through it, the child becomes sensitive to the warmth that streams toward him; the warmth supports all life in him.

But the development of the senses goes far beyond this. There exists also a sense for the feeling of speech. Through this, the child conceives the sound of the spoken word and vibrates to it long before he is able to understand the language. For this reason, it is essential to speak in a clear, full-toned voice in the neighborhood of the child. (I shall give further details of this in connection with learning to speak and the origin of certain diseases.)

Another sense organ gives the possibility of the perception of thoughts and ideas. The "sense of the perception of thoughts," Steiner calls it. It is an accepted idea of our times that we grasp thoughts only by first analysing them, and then building them up again from their parts. Living, unprejudiced experience shows that we apprehend directly and as a whole the ideas and thoughts that are conveyed to us in speech. The appropriate sense organ experiences an idea as a unity, just as we experience a picture as a unity without breaking it up into single forms. For a long time before he gains an intellectual understanding in his soul of ideas and thoughts, the child is already living in the thought life of his surroundings through this sense of thought perception. In the same way the eye lives in the multiplicity of colors long before those contours are grasped that later become the sky, the meadows and the trees.

Thus it is clear that a child should live in an atmosphere of right thoughts. If an untruth is spoken in the world around it, the child takes in harmful thought forces through its sense of thought perception. Loving thoughts in the mind of its mother will make the child jump for joy. They are as blessed a food for his soul as pure milk is for his body.

The over-intellectual man of today will indignantly demand a proof of this. It is only possible, of course, to observe some of the facts and to investigate them. How often do we see mothers walking with their little children. For some of them it seems to be an irksome duty; slowly and without interest they push the pram along. Some don't think at all; others let their minds wander aimlessly. All kinds of thoughts come and go in their heads—worries about money, about their husbands, or about other people. Look into the eyes of the children whose mothers do everything for them half-mechanically—even though with the best intentions! Their eyes are sad and dull; at the age of six months they may already have lost their wonderful radiance. One can see great disappointment in the look of these children. Everything is mirrored in the eyes, but it may show also in the whole expression of the face, and even in the tone of the skin—whether it looks clear or lifeless.

Another of the senses through which a man can penetrate deeply into his surroundings is that sense whereby he recognizes the essential being of a human individual. Rudolf Steiner called it the sense of perception of the ego, and by this he implied of course the perception of the ego of another being, not that of the observer himself.

The child who is still far from having any consciousness of himself can already penetrate deeply into the being of the adults living around him. With this in mind, one can understand how it is that a child chooses his friends in his own way. The choice often diverges from what the parents would wish or expect. But the child remains up to a point unassailable in his preference for this or that person. He is not influenced by tradition, nor by social considerations! But what does play an important part is whether the given person is wise and warm-hearted—one who has learned from life—or whether he is more superficial. Thus a child may often be drawn to a wise grandmother or grandfather who has grown old in the right way. For a young human being can form an inner relationship with an old one in which there is great mutual understanding. The child, penetrating into his surroundings by means of those senses referred to above, and gradually learning to come back again into his body with all the experience he has gained—this child has something in common with the old man. The latter is now again living more outwardly into his surroundings than in middle life, and, if he has grown old in the right way, has learned to understand what he meets there. He cannot, of course, come back again so easily into his now fragile body as can the child, but he can now consciously understand the wisdom of the world, while the child receives his impressions still more or less unconsciously.

IV

Steiner speaks of another group of senses, whose activity is in the opposite direction to those above described. By means of these, one can experience through certain feelings what is happening within the body. Through the "sense of life," as it is called, man conceives of himself as a unity. An example may make clearer what is meant by this. Imagine someone lying down in the sand near the sea. He exposes himself to the air, which is well warmed by the sun. The healthy body will then experience a feeling of joy and contentment in its own unified and harmonious workings, and it is this feeling that is conveyed by the "sense of life." One can clearly see this contentment in an infant that has been fully satisfied by its feed. But the moment the baby does not get the right amount or the right quality of milk, this inner comfort will be lost. The "sense of life" then conveys only a feeling of discomfort. Upon the impressions received through the sense of life during early childhood will depend later how the adult feels altogether in his soul; whether he is contented and at peace, or is always sour-tempered because there is apparently something in his organism that makes him unsatisfied.

The "sense of movement" gives us knowledge of the movements carried out by our muscles and joints. In physiology, too, the muscular and articular sense is named. By the "sense of movement" Steiner understands that through which the child experiences all movements, from the mere lifting of hands and arms, to the ability to sit, to stand and to move in space. This sense has great importance for the human soul. Through it, we come to feel that we are free beings. This applies only to the adult years; nevertheless, one can understand how essential it is for the child to have the right guidance in using the forces of movement and uprightness. Through no other impulse than that of his own individuality should the child acquire the faculty of walking upright. The soul will feel itself free in later life only if it was allowed to penetrate into the body through its own strength—not through arbitrary manipulations, such as baby exercises. Interferences of this kind may cause, as mentioned before, such enforced immobility as occurs in rheumatic and arthritic diseases. They may also result in an inner lack of freedom. A man who feels himself as if chained to the earth and to the world of matter may owe this to the experience of the "sense of movement" in his childhood, when he was driven too early in life into his limbs, and forced to walk before he was ready for it.

Next comes the "sense of balance." This enables us to keep, for example, to a position we have taken up. What has been said about the "sense of movement" and its connection with the development of freedom in later life holds good even more for this sense. For the faculty of preserving one's physical balance has to an even greater extent its inner counterpart. It is possible, through the activity of this sense organ in childhood, to attain later to a quietude of soul so great that one can, as Steiner puts it, feel oneself as a spiritual being. He who was able, as a child, to develop the sense of balance in the right way, may achieve a human quality that can be considered as a climax of individual development: the ability to experience in inner peace and quietness the working of the spirit. The child anticipates unconsciously perhaps what may happen in later years, and shows the joy with which he strives again and again to achieve uprightness. But the child who is driven too early to the attainment of physical balance will have to suffer for it later in his mind. He will be exposed to the danger of becoming restless and losing that inner peace that is so important to the finding of one's true being. Who will not think, in this connection, of the nerviness and restlessness of the people of our age? How many there are who are not even able to remain alone with themselves, who hurry from one entertainment to the next merely in order to avoid facing their own true being.

One reason for the now prevalent "nerviness" is clearly a wrong education in childhood. The child who is not allowed to achieve uprightness by his own individual effort is robbed, as an adult, of the peaceful awareness in himself of his own spirit.

The sense of touch is another of the senses through which one is made aware of one's own organism. Steiner especially points out that it is always ourselves that we feel in the activity of our sense of touch; we experience purely at the surface of the body, the shifting of our skin and the degree of pressure upon it. Speaking of this sense, he says also, "It is nothing else than a being permeated by the feeling of God, which radiates towards the inner being and is experienced as from without." This statement may seem strange and I shall try to explain it, in the following way. The sense of touch leads us into our own body; whatever approaches us from outside through the sense of touch pushes (quite literally) against our physical being. But we also forget ourselves immediately (provided only that pain is not combined with the sensation of touch) and submerge ourselves in what touches us. If one is able to experience the counterpart in the realm of the soul, then an even higher level is reached than that achieved through the sense of balance. For as a result of an appropriate development, we may become able to feel ourselves completely penetrated by a spiritual being; we may be able to give ourselves up and become the vessel for the Divine. A condition such as this is usually experienced unconsciously at the moment of falling asleep. An instinctive knowledge of this fact seems to exist in some children and probably accounts for certain peculiar actions performed when they are going to sleep. One can often see even in babies the desire to stroke something rhythmically with their fingers before they fall asleep. Some like to touch a soft piece of linen, and this they may go on doing for several years. Or it might be a piece of woolen material, or the soft frock of their doll. Many, again, solve the problem in the simplest way by putting a finger or thumb in their mouth and sucking it. In this way the sensation of touch is doubled, for it is experienced on the finger as well as on the lips and tongue, which are very sensitive. There are even children who combine the two; they put two fingers in their mouth and suck them, and with the other hand hold their piece of woolen material pressed against their cheek. This impulse in children to activate the sense of touch when they are going to sleep seems to be nothing more than a longing to experience the "feeling of God," which the moment they are asleep becomes a reality. If a child goes on wanting to suck his thumb as he gets older, it should draw our attention to the fact that he is not wakened up enough to his surroundings, that he is not occupied enough with them. A child who takes enough interest in the outer world will give up this sucking during the day; just before going to sleep he may still put his thumb quickly into his mouth. Only such a one-sided psychology as psychoanalysis could invent a sexual background for thumb-sucking in early childhood. This thumb-sucking has—in spite of what Freud may say—nothing to do with any erotic satisfaction. What a superficial or prejudiced observation interprets in this way is certainly nothing but a longing in the child to experience the inner activity of the sense of touch leading him to the fringe of sleep. It is, of course, desirable that the child should stop sucking his thumb in the third year and find the world around him more interesting than his own inner experience.

Every teacher should be aware of this fact, for one often finds persisting in children of school age such habits and tendencies as these that are natural to babyhood. If one sees the need in children over three to be always touching things, licking and feeling them with their lips, it points to a lack of right occupations and too drowsy a consciousness. In adults, too, one can observe a falling back into a kind of transformation of a soul condition belonging to early childhood; the passion for chewing gum is probably similar in its origin to thumb-sucking in babyhood.

Finally, we come to the fifth of those that Rudolf Steiner describes as the "inner senses"—the sense of smell. Scents and smell have a deep influence on man. In the activity of smelling, we renounce our own individuality even more completely than in touching. We allow a scent to enter right into ourselves; we open ourselves to it. It is therefore a personal question for everyone as to which of the many scents and smells they like or dislike most. One can experience the feeling of being imbued with a particular scent most easily in the flowering season. One person may love to fill himself with the scent of lilac—as is described in "Dorian Gray." (Wilde was a writer who had an intimate relation to the world of smelling.) For others it may be violets, jasmin, lilies of the valley, orange blossom, rosemary or lavender that give them their favorite scent. There is really something of a moral background in the connection people may have with certain scents. A most beautiful memory can be linked with a particular scent, as well as a painful one with an offensive smell. In our times, however, people seem to have lost much of these subtle feelings, as witness the scents of perfumes, soaps, hair lotions and so forth that fill our nostrils in a theater, ballroom or concert-hall, without apparently arousing any objections in our fellow men. The smells permeating the flats and houses of his patients reveal much to the medical practitioner about the characters of the inhabitants. There is the smell of poverty, of uncleanliness, greediness, weariness, orderliness, and of many other qualities.

Steiner even says that the experiences connected with the sense of smell through which one becomes united with a scent are similar to mystical experiences. For the essential quality of the mystic is in his faculty of uniting himself completely with something that penetrates his inner being—in the mystical experience, the Divine.*

Through a bad-smelling atmosphere much harm can be done in childhood. Bad smells should be kept away from the baby's cot, and soaps and dusting powders with a strong scent should not be used. It need hardly be mentioned that the smell of uncleanliness is detrimental. But also, the steam from the kitchen, loaded with the smells of meat and fish, should be kept away from the baby. The influence of bad smells in early childhood may lead in later life to difficulties in acquiring the right moral feelings. In connection with the "backward" child, Rudolf Steiner points out that children with a tendency to enjoy a bad smell reveal through this symptom some deeper moral

---

* To prevent misunderstanding, I must emphasize that it is not my intention to write for or against mysticism. But the fact of such mystical experiences as are described in the literature of the Middle Ages is here considered to be a reality and not a mere fantasy.

defect. As an example, he mentions children with a liking for the smell of paraffin.

Finally, I would draw attention to that delicate scent that usually comes from a well-kept baby. When one remembers what a pleasure it is to experience this, one cannot help wishing that the scent were not so often lost to us through some clever feat of toilet on the part of the mother.

V

To sum up, then, this account of the world of the senses, it is clear that we have to distinguish between those that are directed toward the outer world, such as the sense of sight, and those directed toward the inner world, such as the "sense of life."

During the years of development, the outwardly directed senses have the greatest importance for the building up of the body. Everything that comes from outside leaves its trace in the life forces, and in this way has its reaction upon the finer construction of the organism. What is brought to the human organs at this early stage may show its consequences many years later. The "inner senses" such as the "sense of life" and the "sense of balance" have a similar effect on the body, but they also have a special influence on the psychological side of development in the child, and later in the adult.

To give an idea of the manifoldness of the senses, it was necessary to mention each one, even if only briefly. But it should never be forgotten that by degrees they all come to work harmoniously together. There are, indeed, pronounced interconnections between some of them. Three, for instance—the senses of hearing, of speech and of the perception of the other ego—are particularly closely linked together. In our experience of life it is so that what we hear through our ears, how speech sounds to us, and what we learn of the personality who has spoken to us together form a unity. On the basis of the knowledge of this close connection between several senses, it becomes abundantly clear that record-player, radio and television are real enemies to the right development of children. The world should be brought to them only in natural truthfulness. It is quite easy to understand that to the spoken word belongs a personality. So that in their apprehension of speech, at least three senses should be active, to say nothing of the eyes, through which the speaker should also be seen. We must, then, avoid offering to children a mutilated world just at the time when their senses have to learn to work in an harmonious way. Those people who live the natural life of primitive tribes were much frightened at first when they were allowed to listen to recordings. For them, the whole apparatus was an instrument of the devil. Why? Because they could hear a voice sounding from something without a soul, and music without the human being who belongs to it. The sense for the perception of the other ego remained unsatisfied; the world seemed robbed of something essential. These primitive people thought, of course, that only a devil could be the cause of such a mutilation.

The child—and here I refer especially to the first seven years—becomes more and more used to meeting a falsified world. This is bound to cause harm. The cinema brings about a disharmony in the activity of the sense organs. It disturbs the formation of the right relationship between eyes, ears and the senses for the perceptions of thoughts, speech and the other ego. The climax of the chaos brought into the life of the senses is now reached through the influence of television. This invention also is responsible for preventing at least five of the senses from working together in their natural relationship, and there is the added disadvantage that it penetrates even more deeply into the daily life than does the cinema. This is because it can be enjoyed in comfort at home, and in the family circle.

Although this book deals only with young children, some further remarks on this subject will here be interpolated. It cannot but be of advantage to point out some of the consequences that radio, recordings, cinema and television have on the lives of children, since not even the youngest is always shielded from the influence of these inventions. In all of them that one sense is excluded through which we have to learn to know the other person. The lack of a deeper insight into the human character has become a special illness of our times. Nowadays, people judge their fellowmen in the most superficial and wrong way. One of the real reasons for this is that the sense that experiences the other individual is brought far too little into use, and indeed is almost paralyzed by modern technique. Just as a blind eye cannot be the mediator of color and form, so a man with a kind of paralyzed sense for the perception of the other ego cannot clearly grasp another personality. What is the use of preaching love and understanding for our fellowmen if the sense that enables us to achieve it is systematically destroyed by modern civilization. There are many modern schools that boast of introducing the great achievements of mankind, and this because they do not shrink from using recordings, radio, cinema and television in education!

Unfortunately, through such a practice the children are educated to ignorance of the human being, and many evils of the present time are rooted in that ignorance. More and more professional men—teachers, doctors, artists, scientists, politicians and so on—come from their training with little or no understanding for the real human being.

VI

Following the description of the way in which a child gradually learns to use its body and to enter into the world with its will, and also of how the senses reveal the earth to it, it may be of interest to go into the question of the play of small children and their toys.

As soon as the child begins to grasp things firmly, he can be given a simple wooden doll—one which is but broadly indicated as to its form. The impact of this toy on the sense organs should give real joy to the baby. It is important that beauty should be one of its attributes, however simple it may be. Even the rattle, usually the first toy, should have an artistic form. It should be spherical. Children love the form of a ball because they feel related to it especially in so far as their head is concerned. The head has brought this form from the whole cosmos. It makes the child happy to meet something with a form to which its head is connected; something with which it is familiar. The color of the rattle should be delicate and no object should be painted on it. It is difficult to decide what is the best material; wood, perhaps, if possible, not celluloid, plastic or rubber. Wood always has about it something warm and alive. Beautiful eastern rattles are still to be found made of ivory with filigree work like lace. Preferable to the little balls of wood or stone, which give a toneless sound, are small bells made of silver.

95

Very young children often play with their own small fingers, which they touch, look at, and as already mentioned, put into their mouths.

One can observe something that seems strange in some babies from a few weeks after birth up to nine months and even longer. It is not merely play, but should nevertheless be described. These babies appear to be interested in the shadows made by themselves or by other people. At first it seemed difficult to find an explanation for this. The children give the impression of being quite fascinated when they see shadows; they show more interest in them than in many other things. In quite another connection, Rudolf Steiner makes a remark that seems to help one to understand this phenomenon. He speaks of the seer, who may for the first time see the spirit in his own shadow thrown by the sun. "The body checks the light but not the spirit; and in the shadow thrown by the body the spirit can be discovered. It is for this reason that primitive tribes, who have always had clair- voyant sight, have called the shadow also the soul; they say 'without a shadow—without a soul'." Is it not then likely that the baby, who is still so much connected with its spiritual home, is able to see in the shadow on the wall something spiritual that the adults cannot see? This interest in shadows may last many months, and disappears as the child becomes more and more absorbed in the physical world.

Toward the end of the first year, it is quite good to give the baby a rag doll, whose face is only just indicated with a few lines or points. The whole doll must be colored, and should show an artistic harmony. Just as the child is stimulated by his food to build up his physical body, so is he stimulated by this primitive doll to bring into play the forces of imagination. Steiner has clearly indicated that such a toy rouses man's powers of fantasy and keeps them alive in later years.

Soft toys (animals) and animals made of wood may be given to the child when he is really able to walk. It is important in these present times to say a few words about such animals. They should be shaped in a simple way, and any kind of caricature must be strictly avoided. Those unhappy creatures, therefore, who have their origin in the Mickey Mouse films should not appear at all in the nursery. These film stars created by Disney have lost all those soul-qualities that belong to every animal, and are loved by children; the dry human intellect has here put itself, with a presumptuous wittiness, above the animal. Such a "zoology" cannot but be fatal for the child. It is worth mentioning that Steiner speaks occasionally of two kinds of animals that should not be given as toys—the monkey and the bear. A little thought reveals the reasons for this. The figure of the ape is a caricature of man when he is hardened in his being. Clearly the child can benefit nothing from having before him, as a toy, the form of a disfigured and caricatured man; this would not help to give life to the imagination. I puzzled for some time over what it is about the bear without being able to solve the question. Finally, a remark made in quite another connection seemed to me to be helpful. Willy Sucher in his book *Isis-Sophia* writes about the bear. There he points out that the bear is an animal that stands firmly on the earth, and moves about cleverly and quickly. The bear is too strongly connected with the earth, and this indeed is revealed by its form. Sucher adds also that human beings who have the impulse to press too deeply into matter, thus forgetting the spirit, are represented in legends as bears. This is certainly true, and the idea appears also in

Grimm's fairy tales. There the bears are usually enchanted princes who have to be redeemed from their earthly heaviness. With just this heaviness, the child should not unite himself at any early age. No toy animals at all should be given to the child before he is able to walk. It is much more important for him to watch people who have already achieved what he has to learn to become an upright walking creature. It is striking to see the way children watch the walking of adults before they can walk themselves. They never tire of looking at the feet of the grown-ups who are going about them. With the searching gaze of a scientist, they try to find out how it is that people are able to move about. From this it becomes obvious how wrong it would be to show them toy animals at this time. But as soon as the baby is walking freely, many animals can be given to it so long as they are made of wood or soft materials. A certain stage of development has now been reached by the playing child. In the second and third year he should be given things that encourage him to move his limbs. The doll should be big so that the child can do with it what he does himself and should be movable enough that it can sit down for meals, be laid down at night, and so on. The child should have a little cart to lead, and an animal to pull along on a string as he walks, and he may also have a ball to throw about.

These toys, which involve an activity on the part of children, serve to develop the will. At the same time the senses should also be nurtured through the beauty of the toys. One can achieve this quite simply by the use of pure colors, in the ball as well as in the carved animals and the toy cart on wheels.

For the development of the child's imagination, it is of great value to have movable toys. They should, however, have no complicated mechanisms such as are made at present. But with a little wooden dog on wheels, for instance, one can try to make its legs and tail move. The pictures that are implanted in the child's soul by such movements have something in them of the old wood-cuts. Their simple form brings it about that the child adds something to them himself out of an inner effort. Just this effort makes the soul more alive and inventive in later years. Thus it is essential to keep away from the child all those ugly clockwork toys made of iron, tin or plastic that can be wound up to move by themselves, to say nothing of the electric trains with which fathers and sons love to play. Good examples of right and suitable toys have been made by the older pupils in Rudolf Steiner schools in their handicraft lessons.

VII

In the games which he loves to play after he can walk, the child tries to invent for himself what he needs for his own development. He will try over and over again to attain to certain faculties. What for him is exercise and learning often seems to the adult to be a game, and in a way it is also a game. A child may want, for instance, to climb up a bank. He feels that he cannot overcome the slope. He will try several times to climb up, generally falling down and having to start again from the beginning. Such practicing as this will be done in a good mood, with a laugh at each fall. Until it is three the day of a child is filled with such efforts, and the grown-up must have the right understanding for the importance of what it is that the child is doing. An interesting game, of which children never tire in the first years of life, is that of hide and seek. There is in that game the expression of something that is among the most fundamental of the processes in the human being. The task of a child is to find his best way to earth. This becomes more and more possible if the things of the outer world that are met by the child are harmonized with the inner soul world. But the child's soul is still in a labile state. Now he is occupied by the world of the senses, which takes hold of him, and in the next moment the world of his inner will is excited and the soul penetrates deeply into the body. In this way there is a continuous approaching and withdrawing of the soul to and from the body. It is this activity that the child imitates in the game of hide and seek.

Another game children love has a similar background. This consists in collecting things together, and then distributing them again. They like, for example, to put all their toys into a shopping basket, and then when they have packed it full, to hand them over again to somebody, one by one. They often do the same thing when they are left by themselves—spreading all the things out and then fetching them back again. In such a way are processes that take place in the living organism transformed into a game. Only think of how children love to build something up out of pieces of wood. They will construct a little tower and then suddenly push the whole thing down again. The undiscerning adult will quite likely say, "Oh, what a pity that you've destroyed it." But the little boy or girl, quite unconcerned with the reproof, will make another tower only to destroy it again in the same way. The process of life in our bodies consists also of a continual breaking down and building up of matter. Anyone who looks after a child at this age must admire the wisdom of these games if he observes them against the background of this knowledge. On the other hand he will see to it that the playing does not turn into mere senseless activity.

It should not be forgotten that "sense" is here meant from the point of view of the child, not from that of the adult, who is prejudiced by his grown-up intellectuality. The adult point of view is unfortunately imposed in a system of education, such as the Montessori method, which is too much thought out; this system has encroached even into early babyhood. The dangerous factor in this and other methods is that the intention stands in the foreground to inculcate something into the child. It is assumed in nearly all these methods that the small child also has something to "learn" through education. There is often the ruling idea that one can educate a small child in just the same way as one trains a dog: whatever is drummed into him, he will remember and know.

In reality, of course, it is necessary to pay attention with ever-increasing understanding to what a child develops out of himself and what this means. It will then become clear what should be done, and what guidance given. Children who are not spoiled by their surroundings usually know well enough in the first years what is a good and suitable toy for them. They often throw away what is bad for them or show little interest in it. But close observation is necessary in order to find out these things.

VII

THE GATEWAY OF FEELING

I

To follow the way in which the feeling soul of the child strives to incarnate is more difficult than in the case of the thinking or the willing soul. Once the gateways of the senses are opened, there streams through them comparatively easily what comes from the inner or from the outer physical world. The sense perceptions are inscribed by way of the sense organs and their appropriate nerves, but the impulses of the will strive toward the periphery and are discharged in the movements of the limbs. The nerves belonging to the sense organs lead finally to the brain, the instrument of thinking. They are, from the evolutionary point of view, very old; they point back to something that belongs to the past, whereas the will points to the future, to something that will only later shape itself. Whatever I *will* do is not in the present, or it would no longer be necessary to make an effort of the will.

It is quite different with feeling. Feeling belongs to the present, and develops itself at each moment anew. If one meditates upon a feeling, it is already gone; if one anticipates it, it is not yet there. In the first years the life of feeling is very much in a state of development. It is as if it were at this stage overpowered by the two polarities of the soul, by perception and will. It has to grow up between them. Thus Steiner could point out that the child is wholly a sense organ (he connects himself completely, through the twelve sense organs, with the world, which then becomes perceptible to him from inside and from outside), and he is also wholly a being of will (since he follows his own impulses without inner restraint). Because these two realms of sense perception and of will are so closely joined in the first three years, the child is at that age an imitative being. He *sees* how his mother holds the spoon, and immediately *wants* to do it in the same way. Or the father may strike the table with his fist; the child sees this, takes it in and it flows directly into the sphere of the will; the picture that has penetrated into the child then initiates a will impulse and the child also strikes the table.

Or again, a child goes into a meadow, intending to run to the apple tree. At that moment a dog appears. The child is drawn by the sight of the dog, the apple tree is forgotten, and he runs to the dog. Then he hears the clucking of a hen, and finds the sound so interesting that he lets the dog go and turns his steps towards the fowl. There is at first not much feeling connected with these activities. Indeed, there would hardly be time enough between them for any feelings to develop at all. Only when an obstacle comes in the way, let us say a bush, then there occurs a congestion of the will that stops the child from fulfilling his desire. The congestion causes an antipathy—perhaps even a pain in the soul. Suddenly, this wild pain is felt, which no thinking

103

can cool down as might happen in later years. The child cries, he feels the discomfort resulting from the obstacle in his whole body; and so, according to his temperament he will either throw himself down before the blocked road in a frantic fit of rage, or stand helpless with tears in his eyes. Such an outburst of anger or sorrow often shows the connection of feeling with the breathing and circulation. In some children, breathing stops at such a moment; they become bluish in the face and make rhythmic jerks with their limbs until they gain the strength to send out the air from their lungs where it was imprisoned. Children cry easily because the physical instrument of their feelings does not become fully organized until some years have elapsed. What should the grown-up do? If possible, he should remove the obstacle and end the child's pain. Or he may look for something else to show to the little being so that its attention is diverted by some other sense perception. The silliest thing that can be done—and so-called unsentimental mothers choose this method only too often—is to hit the child to bring it to its senses. What happens then? The painful feeling is increased and the obstacle is not only not removed, it now becomes insurmountable. The child only sees now—from outside—the rage and anger of the adult. This is an undesirable diversion, and it may happen that the child—in an imitative reaction—hits the mother back. There are two possible consequences to this. Either the mother may reconsider the situation and see the failure of her educational attempt; then her anger cools down, she is ashamed and tries to calm the child's fury; or she may feel moral indignation at the bad boy or girl who lifts its hand against its mother; her rage increases and the little being is given

104

another thrashing, until it has—as the weaker party—to give in, and can find no other expression for its sorrow than by sobbing. Such scenes can be witnessed daily at any street corner! The younger the child the worse is the effect of this lack of understanding in the grown-up. The ideally slow and unimpeded taking hold of the body by the feelings is hindered, and through such experiences, the child may grow up into a person suffering from depressions or even an organically damaged rhythmic organism.

The life of feelings develops slowly, is at first little differentiated and goes from one extreme to the other of the scale.

Feeling is based on the rhythmic processes, such as breathing and blood-circulation. These rhythms are at first irregular. They gradually become more balanced as the differentiation of the feelings takes place. A regular rhythm in everyday life is of help to the child in the harmonizing of the feelings. One rhythm, that between sleeping and waking life, should be especially strictly observed. After the night's sleep and the activity of the morning, the child must have another rest-time before lunch, at least for the first three years, and if possible even longer. A short rest in the afternoon may also be desirable for some children for several years. Meals must always be punctual.

Children at this age love all repetitions in games. This helps to improve the breathing, regulate the circulation and form sound organs of feeling. Even external observation reveals how much the streaming breath and blood are influenced by the waves of feeling. A child who looks up in wonder at a ball thrown high in the air opens his mouth wide, holds his breath

105

and grows paler for a moment; then he may take a deep breath and become flushed in the face. Children will often hold their breath when they are confronted by something new.

The rhythmic repetitions in games and daily life have the effect of restoring regularity. Their good influence is unconsciously demanded by the child. Rhythm brings health to breathing and circulation.

The fundamental feelings in the first years are joy and sorrow, which reveal themselves in laughing and crying. There is no room for these things in the young baby. The newly born has not even the tears that belong to human sorrow at its disposal, and opinions differ as to the time when it begins to smile. This difference is merely due to the fact that some babies smile at two weeks, others at six weeks or later. Both expressions of feeling are borne on the wings of breathing: laughing on an intensified exhalation, crying on an intensified inhalation. The rhythm of breathing is conveyed to the blood-rhythm in a child much more than in an adult, and so the heart receives, by way of these rhythms, the two kinds of feelings that live so near together in early childhood.

A physiological description of these conditions can be given, which may sound less strange to a scientific ear. That is, that in young children the breathing has a much greater influence than in later life. The pulse is slowed down and becomes calmer through deep exhalation (as in laughing), whereas deep inhalation (as in crying or sobbing) causes an acceleration, and the pulse is excited. One sees from the quick fluctuations between laughing and crying that occur in a child how little he is able to master the world of rhythm (and with it the feelings). But the feelings are received and registered by the heart; there they are experienced. One can localize them there when, for instance, the heart is aching with sorrow, or leaping with joy. Man's most sublime feeling—true love—is also felt in the heart itself. Love, too, is always connected with joy and sorrow, with laughing and crying; in love, just as in the child, the feelings are bounded by laughing and crying. It comes easily to a poet to describe such things, which a more scientific mind can hardly grasp with its thoughts. Thus the great poet Friedrich Rueckert has written a poem, *Laughing and Weeping*, well-known through the song of Schubert, who gave even greater depth to the words with his music.

> Laughing and weeping at every season
> Has often in love its different reason
> Oft in the morning I laugh with joy
> And why I weep yet
> At the evening's set
> I do not know why, I do not know why.

> Weeping and laughing at every season
> Has often in love its different reason.
> Oft in the evening I weep for pain.
> Why the morning thereafter
> I waken with laughter
> I must ask you, O heart, I must ask you, O heart.

II

In small children between one and two years, and even a few months before the first year, one can see a remarkable kind of memory at work. The ability to remember seems at this age to be different from what it becomes in later years. Think of a child who passes a door that is not closed but left on the latch; he invents for himself a game of opening and closing the door, opening and closing. Having done this one day, the child will try to repeat the game every time he comes past the same door. The working of this kind of memory will be understood when one bears in mind the above described relationship between the three functions of the soul—thinking, feeling and willing. On the first occasion, the child sees the door, then touches and moves it. The perception of the door sinks directly into the region of the will, hardly touching at all the feeling sphere. In this way, the perception is written, so to speak, into the forces of life, from which the impulses of will then directly emerge. These "life forces," which have to do with the forming of the physical body, together constitute another, invisible body; it is this invisible body that becomes the bearer of memory a few years later. Steiner called these invisible forces the etheric forces.

In every human being they are organized into an ether body, and have to do, as mentioned, with the faculty of memory. But in the earliest period of life, roughly up to the third year, memory works differently. This has been shown by the example of the door. Such a method of recollection is possible at that age because sense perception and will are still in immediate connection with each other, at moments almost becoming one. An illustration taken from the world of the animals may make this clearer. It must be emphasized that comparisons of the animals with man has led to much confusion of thought as to the true conception of man himself. Nevertheless there is a certain similarity between memory in young children and in some animals. The act of remembering, as demonstrated in the example of the door, is closely related to the working of the memory in a dog. Dogs have a good sense of hearing and a particularly keen sense of smell. Everything they perceive through either of these sense organs penetrates at once into the region of the will so that a given perception is followed each time by the same action. It is for this reason that the dog can be trained. It gets wind of the fox and is off at once on the hunt. Or it smells at a piece of clothing, and follows the scent until it gets its victim. It hears a noise and at once it has to bark. The essential fact for our consideration is that in such an animal, as in the child, the sense perception flows immediately into the will impulse. In the dog—and this is important—rhythm and feeling have little influence on such an activity. The soul forces are in a way similarly balanced in the little child, and there we see the peculiar kind of remembering I have described. From the age of three this gradually changes in the measure that all three faculties of the soul become harmonized.

III

While he is still unable to express his wants and needs, a child will often suffer acutely because he is not understood. He wants to do many things, and wishes for many things—but cannot say so. The observant person who has care of the child should gradually become so familiar with all the emotions of the growing being that he or she can quickly guess his aims and thoughts. Only remember how long a small child has sometimes to go on crying before the adult realizes that hunger is the cause, or thirst or cold, or heat. Although it may seem difficult to understand how, a clever observer can soon recognize each one of the baby's longings. One can see, for instance, that some children, when they want a drink, draw air into their mouths with protruded lips.

Adults should always remember how difficult life would become for them if they were in a country whose language they did not understand. Most of their wants would remain unfulfilled if nobody understood them. Yet a baby is in just the same position so that most people do not understand it.

In the same way that learning to walk is a big step forward in the development of the child's will, so is learning to speak a most important stage in the unfolding of the world of feelings. The appearance of a new soul faculty can be observed when the child forms, on the stream of breathing, its Ah's and Oh's. The vowel sounds uttered by little children can inform a sensitive ear of the feelings they want to express. How much astonishment, admiration and joy can be heard in an Ah! The differentiation is often conveyed by strength of tone, repetition and the duration of the sound. A different feeling is expressed by the Oh-sound. There is often pain in it, but also some degree of control. The startled feeling that is conveyed by an exclamation such as "Heavens!" sounds milder when, with the Oh-sound, it becomes "Oh, Heavens!" These interjections are generally considered to be the beginning of speech in children. Even in the way in which they begin to form the consonants a shade of feeling can still be found. It is difficult to learn to walk as an upright being—but it is even more difficult and more complicated to learn to speak. The child never tires of repeating again and again just those sounds he hears. At first it all occurs in a dream-like way, just as do the feelings. A good opportunity for observation is the time before the child falls asleep. Then it will practice, for instance, the L-sound, joining it to the Ah (as it is pronounced in father). In that Ah, the stream of exhalation unfolds itself; the sounding L endows the breathing with wings that carry the soul from waking to dreaming. Sometimes, if there is some disturbance of the silence, one can hear the child's rumbling R rising angrily from within like distant peals of thunder.

The expression of feelings is to be heard in many different syllables, and it is this that makes the efforts to speak so charming at this time of life. The feeling quality grows less and less as, after the age of three, a more intellectual element penetrates the speech. But the feelings come out especially clearly when the child calls to certain people whom it knows. An abundance of loving devotion lives in the over and over again repeated "Ma-ma" or "Pa-pa". Later on, in about a year's time, this particular sweetness of sound gradually disappears. Whoever is able to penetrate intimately into the essence of the child's speaking will immediately recognize how the vowels sound out from the depths of feeling in the soul. The vowels come out on the exhaled air and at first children more or less sing them. This is especially so with happy children, who sing out their Ah's in the evening and when they are in bed. Listening to this singing reminds one of what Rudolf Steiner once said about the origin of language. "In ancient times in the earthly development of man, there was no differentiation in his manifestation of speech and tone into song and speech; *both were one.* What one can say about the human primordial speech could be expressed in the following way: this primordial human speech is a primordial song."

It becomes obvious, then, that in learning to speak, children repeat the whole development of speech in mankind.

111

IV

In the formation of the consonants, the stream of exhaled air is interrupted; barriers are put in its path by movements of the lips, teeth or tongue. Take for instance, a short word: up. Here the movement of the lips that corresponds to the P-sound puts a momentary stop to the stream of air. Through these differing interruptions, different shades of feeling are conveyed. A child of under two years who can hardly speak may do the following. This example is true in all its details. In the evening, before going to sleep, he sounds and sings over and over again in a loud clear voice the vowel Ah. Suddenly a train passes by near the house. Now the child is familiar with the noise of the engine during the day. In his darkened room as soon as he hears the sound of the moving train through the drawn curtains, he interrupts his Ah song with three puffs—F–F–F; then he goes back to the Ah. Into the pure feeling of joy expressed in the Ah, a nuance of unrest is brought, sounding in the F, as of something in quick flight. In this instance, not only are the feelings manifested in the sound, but something else as well; the child's inner experience of feeling is interrupted by an outside event, to which he reacts with his F–F–F. He tries to imitate the language the train speaks. One can feel from this that the consonant has a certain power in itself. By sounding the F, the child wants to reproduce the essential being of the engine. One step farther and we can understand Rudolf Steiner's explanation of the meaning of consonants in speech. To him each consonant has a particular spiritual content such as is also embodied in the language as a whole. Just as the child finds in the F an expression of the external world, so once did the gods pronounce their own sounds.

112

Imagine now that not only does the child imitate the train with his F–F–F, but that he can create it anew with the sound! When the F streams out of his mouth, an engine and trucks are re-created; in this way one can come to a true comparison with the old power of speech in the gods. Such a consideration may help us to understand one aspect of the deep and mysterious utterance in the Gospel, "In the beginning was the Word . . ." The sounds were at this time really living, and had the power of creation. This is recalled again and again in Genesis, where we read, "And the Lord God *said.*" In *saying* he becomes the Creator. Man himself was created by the power of the heavenly Word. Man became a living soul through the fact that God breathed "into his nostrils the breath of life."

To bring together more details about the connection between speech and the origin of man would lead us too far away from our subject. I would, however, point out the importance of the consonants. Each consonant may be considered as the essential emanation from a particular spiritual formative force. That same force, for instance, which forms the R-sound, has to do with the creation of the larynx.

In ancient times people knew not only that man owes his form to the influences of the constellations of the Zodiac, but also that the consonants of the languages have their origin in these stars.

Recall once again how the feelings experienced in the soul resound directly in the vowels. These vowel sounds are then interrupted by the consonantal sounds corresponding to the different parts of the organism. So there can be unfolded in the spoken word a great range of feelings—each one expressed through a consonantal interruption originating from, for example, the upper part of the body, the head, or the limbs. There can be no doubt that our feelings are usually influenced and tinged by the different parts of our body. If there arises in our soul a feeling of joy because of some success, a sick heart can overshadow this joy with anxiety. This, which can happen even in a grown-up person, is much stronger in a child, when the freely rising feeling is differentiated, in speaking, by the interruptions of the consonants. To make this clearer, imagine that the child expresses his joy in the Ah-sound (as in car or hard). Now the T-sound is the consonant that belongs to the forces of the heart. (In the Zodiac, the heart, and the T-sound are related to the Lion.) Suppose that the child has a healthy heart, and has learnt from his surroundings the beautiful T-sounds; then he will express pleasure with TA or ATA or TATA, long before he is able to speak properly. Such sounds spoken out will help the child and lift up his heart. But if the people round the child pronounce their T's in a lazy way, then the baby's mouth will speak lazily too. The badly pronounced T will not free his heart as it should do. This may lead to a slight congestion in the heart. It will right itself, of course, but if the condition is repeated over and over again, damage may result; the true cause of this will lie in the careless speaking of adults.

So far as the vowels are concerned, the child can partly discover them for himself, but this is hardly possible with the consonants. For their formation the help of the grown-ups is necessary. With the support of the grown-ups, the child can, through imitation, find the language that becomes the gateway of the feelings. When the child hears the language clearly spoken, then fine vibrations will be the more readily brought about in the appropriate parts of his organism. An educated

114

adult with an intimate awareness of speech will feel his whole body responding with pleasure to a beautiful and resounding way of speaking, but rather he will feel oppressed and restricted when he hears a lazy speech without character. It is a real danger for a child if the people who live with him imitate his childish language instead of speaking correctly. For his whole body vibrates in harmony with the sounds of speech, especially at this time when his feeling life is first born. So a silly imitation of his own shortcomings will create an oppression, and can even harm the physical organs. Of course, these bad results hardly ever show themselves immediately in the child. But in later life, weaknesses may appear that are caused by such mistakes in upbringing. In the light of the whole relation and connection of these facts, it becomes easier to understand why Rudolf Steiner said, "It is really so that something that may be diagnosed in later life as a weak digestion can be understood when we hear that the patient had as a small baby a nurse who made herself too childish."

Language is the instrument and the gateway through which the feeling soul of man finds its way into the body, just as the will can enter through the limbs and metabolism into the child's organism, and the thinking soul through the sense organs and the nerves.

VIII

THE AWAKENING OF THE EGO

I

As soon as the child has acquired the faculty of communicating more easily with his surroundings by means of language, his life of feeling becomes more varied and deep. His breathing—the giving and taking of which exhalation and inhalation consist—begins now to develop in the right way. Think once again of how difficult it must be for a child to have some special wish, but no possibility of expressing it; or to observe something, and be unable to recount it. As an example only, I may mention something of which Edmund Gosse writes in his autobiography, "Father and Son":

I am seated alone in my baby chair at a dinnertable set for several people. Somebody brings in a leg of mutton, puts it down close to me, and goes out. I am again alone, gazing at two low windows, wide open upon a garden. Suddenly, noiselessly, a large, long animal (obviously a greyhound) appears at one windowsill, slips into the room, seizes the leg

116

of mutton and slips out again. When this happened I could not yet talk. The accomplishment of speech came to me very late, doubtless because I never heard young voices. Many years later, when I mentioned this recollection, there was a shout of laughter and surprise. "That, then, was what became of the mutton! It was not you, who, as your Uncle A. pretended, ate it up in the twinkling of an eye bone and all!"

Now imagine what torture it must be for a child to know about something and yet not be free to tell of it!

At the end of the second year, when the rhythmic system becomes a more harmonious part of the human organism, an important change takes place in the head through the development of speech.

I have shown earlier how quickly the head grows as compared with the other parts of the body. The development of sense organs, nerves and brain is almost completed towards the middle of the third year. At this time, those forces that have to do with the building of the brain, the bones of the head, and all its other organs, become to a certain extent free for other work. It is the time, round about two and a half years, when all the milk teeth have been cut.

The forming of the physical body in accordance with an invisible, but for that no less real plan goes on step by step. As soon as one part of the body is completed, the still existing forces, having finished this one task, are ready to take over another. These growth forces have been named by Rudolf Steiner the etheric forces. I have already mentioned them in connection with memory. They form, in each human being, the etheric body. Every individual has his own etheric body, which contains in itself the plan of the human form. A few months after the end of the second year, those living forces that are connected with the head become gradually freed, and so the child becomes gradually more able to think. But the thinking at this age is quite different from that of adults. The thoughts are formed in pictures and are always imaginative, never abstract. The child cannot understand us if we say "great" or "big." For him, a house is big, or a horse, or his father. He thinks only in such pictures as these. This is true of children up to their fifth year, and I shall mention later the importance of taking it into consideration in their education. One thing only must now be made absolutely clear concerning an occurrence at about the end of the third year. This is a great moment in one's life, and the change takes place almost in one leap.

Through the gateway of the senses the child is now open towards the outer world. Pictures can come through the sense organs into the soul, and it gradually becomes possible for the child to preserve them. Picture-imaginations are thus formed, and the first birth of thinking takes place.

Through the gateway of the will the child is now open towards his inner being; he knows how to use his body and to move his limbs; how to move in response to an impulse of will and how to use his arms if he wants to grasp something.

Meanwhile the rhythm of breathing and circulation has established itself harmoniously between the two extremes of the head organization on the one side and the metabolic-limb system on the other. In this breathing and circulation, the gateway of feeling has developed, and through the unfolding of language the child now finds an expression for things that before have remained hidden. It is at this moment in life that man now reveals himself for the first time as an individual endowed with the three soul faculties of thinking, feeling and willing. Looking in this way at man it is no longer possible to consider him as a higher animal only, for something completely new has made its appearance: the human individuality. It is thus quite clear why the child is able from this time on—when he is three years old—to speak of himself as real personality. He can now say I, and expresses by this his awareness of himself as a being endowed with an ego. (Before this time, when he used the word I, the child was usually only imitating what he had heard other people say—but now he is fully aware of its meaning.) Rudolf Steiner often cited the poet and philosopher Jean Paul as a man who had gone through the experience of the birth of his ego in complete consciousness when he was three years old.*

All important stages in human life announce themselves by preliminary symptoms in a previous stage of development. What shows itself in the third year as a first birth of the ego is repeated again between the ages of nine and ten—though of course at a different level.

It is important that the experience of the ego at the end of the third year is prepared for by right guidance. Certain principles pointed out by Steiner can be a great help at this time. He states

---

* "I shall never forget the event that took place within me, hitherto narrated to no one, and of which I can give place and time, when I stood present at the birth of my self-consciousness. As a small child I stood at the door of the house one morning, looking towards the wood-pile on my left, when suddenly the inner vision 'I am an I' came upon me like a flash of lightning from heaven and has remained shining ever since. In that moment my ego had seen itself for the first time and forever. Any deception is hardly to be conceived of as possible here, for no narration by outsiders could have introduced additions to an occurrence that took place in the holy of holies of a human being, and of which the novelty alone gave permanence to such everyday surroundings."

119

clearly that in the first years of life, everything that is "imposed by the will of the pedagogue will be refused by the child." The child feels a great longing to imitate, in freedom, all that adults reveal to him of their life, but he will not allow himself to be forced. This is especially obvious during the time before he learns to speak. To give an example, a boy of this age was much too much "educated" by his uncle; the uncle loved the child, but was all the time anxious to influence his will. The child was made to sit in a certain way by the side of his uncle, was not allowed to run about freely in the garden, and so on. He was forever being forced to do something he did not like, and this had a strange result. As soon as the boy attained the power of speech at the age of three he quite consciously refused to have any further connection with his uncle and would not even look at him any longer. All attempts to cajole him were unsuccessful. What does this mean, and what can we learn from it?

First, we must understand why it is that the child at this time resists any pressure that is put upon his will. Why does he so often say "No" to everything he is asked to do? Towards the end of the third year, everything is gradually prepared in such a way that there can really be an experience of the self. Now inner freedom is connected with man's ego. The first spark of that freedom can be kindled at the age of three. This is an important moment, and it can be a great help to the child if one has not tried to force him, if one has left him free—up to a certain natural limit. If the adult really keeps to this, he will gain the confidence of the child. The child will then out of his own impulse go to the grown-up whenever he becomes uncertain of his undertakings. For instance, a small boy, picking leaves and grass with which to feed a calf would turn round each time before he gave the green stuff to the animal to ask his father if he should do it. The child clearly felt a little frightened and needed to be encouraged. He could not speak much at that time, but the question could easily be read from the look in his eyes and understood through the sounds he made. It was sufficient only to nod, or to say, "Yes, go on," and at once he did it. But hardly ever should one urge a child at that age to do something that he doesn't want to do. He experiences it as wonderful if he is not pressed to do something, but is allowed to do it freely. This can give him a feeling of freedom.

Certain outstanding personalities have had at this age experiences like that of Jean Paul. Others have then encountered their particular destiny. As a contemporary example one could mention the famous violinist and composer, Fritz Kreisler, whose inclination and love for music revealed itself quite naturally at the age of three.

His much younger colleague, Yehudi Menuhin, was given, when he was three, his first instrument, a toy violin; this he proceeded to throw down on the floor because it did not give out the sounds he desired to hear. Mozart also was three when he first picked out on the piano certain notes that particularly pleased him. It would seem that his creative musical powers then showed themselves for the first time. Thus can the way of destiny so early indicate a particular direction. But only in a few cases is it so obvious as in these examples.

There are moments in the third year—strange though it may seem—when freedom, the true individuality (experience of the ego) and destiny, all play together into human life for the first time. Few people may remember it, but most have experienced it. Those who have the care of children can, if they are observant enough, be of great help to them.

II

Before I deal with the importance of right guidance in thinking between the third and the fifth years, I would recall again how it comes about that in the third year the child is able to experience himself as a personality. Not until this age is a certain harmony achieved between the three systems—the head, the rhythmic and the metabolic system. At another level, harmony is again established in later years when the forces of growth are finally freed from all parts of the body. This occurs at the age of seven, and the child is then ready for school education.

For an understanding of human life it is important to notice a change that takes place in the early years. At first the child is a united and undivided being. He is wholly a sense organ, as Steiner showed us.* The objects in the world around him he perceives directly as unities. When he looks at a tree, he sees only a tree, and is unaware that it is made up of trunk, branches and leaves. But in the course of the development of human thinking the tendency to analytical perception appears and gradually comes to the fore. It has its right place, of course, in the investigation of the physical world, as witness the marvellous discoveries of science. But, the analytical method is not confined

---

* "In the first epoch of life before the changing of teeth, the child is as it were wholly a sense-organ; this you should take in the most literal sense."

122

to the realm of science, and the danger arises when it is made use of in education in early childhood.

It is most important for anyone whose task it is to educate a child to observe how gradually there is an unfolding of the body, the growth forces, the soul life, even of the mind and spirit. He will have to be prepared to do the right thing at the right time, so that the unity of the personality entrusted to him is preserved.

III

How this is done may be described in connection with thinking. As was mentioned above, the power of thought is gained by the child from the third year on through the freeing at that time of the life forces of the head organism. At first, the thoughts are only in picture-form. The child does not grasp abstract concepts. It is for this reason that numbers should never be introduced before the fifth year, at the earliest. One should not make the child count, or repeat those meaningless nursery rhymes in which numbers are used.* He will be driven by these into a sphere for which he is not yet mature or fitted. (This does not mean of course that one would not be able to teach the child to count or even to reckon—merely that it is harmful to do it too early.)

At this early period in life, it is much better to say, "Here is a

---

* I am thinking of:

> One, two
> Buckle my shoe
> Three, four
> Knock at the door
> Five, six
> Pick up the sticks, etc.

red rose, here a yellow rose and here a white rose." This is quite enough. For an adult of today, it will not only be difficult to follow such a rule as this; it will even be apt to seem pedantic. More incomprehensible still will it be to the modern mind if one emphasizes—and seriously emphasizes—that the child should not have to do with anything abstract in his play, even in later years. We must be clear about this. Some toys may have an abstract quality and others, even those of a similar type, may stimulate the imagination. Just think of those simple painted wooden dolls that were once made in beautiful colors. Their eyes consisted only of little points, and their limbs were barely indicated. First there was a big doll, and this could be pulled in half. Inside there was revealed a smaller one, made and painted in the same way. The second again could be opened, and a third one appeared, and this was repeated perhaps five or six times. Russian and Polish toys of this kind were beautifully colored in such a way that one could see at once that the biggest doll was the great-grandmother, the second the grandmother, the third the mother, and so on. With such a toy as this, a child was occupied in a good way. It was a colorful and beautiful piece of work. The child enjoyed it, and at the same time his etheric forces were suitably stimulated. But take the toy made on the same principle: a big cube containing many smaller and smaller cubes. Here is an abstract, dry and harmful toy, for the cube is something abstract. There is no life in it, and the child is subjected to forces that harden him far too early. The faculty of thinking in pictures is weakened by such a toy. Abstract thinking is developed too early and the body feels the harm of it in later years.

Unfortunately, such contrivances as the nest of cubes, and

others like it, are given to children in the Montessori kindergartens. The teachers start with the assumption that one should make the child learn as soon as possible through his play. He is taught to develop a sense for numbers and a sense for space, and he learns reading and writing long before the right school age.*

As a means to quick learning, all kinds of solid and hollow geometrical bodies are used. These do the same kind of harm, only in a more concentrated way, as the nest of cubes. An educational method that begins with wrong toys will surely proceed to further mistakes after the third year. Among such mistakes is the desire to train the child's memory in a quite arbitrary way by making him learn verses by heart and repeat stories that have been told to him. Bringing anything to do with numbers to the child's consciousness is equally wrong. It is harmful to train the memory before the beginning of the true school age. It must be left to the child to remember what he can.

Think of that first kind of memory in the child, when the sense impressions penetrate directly into the region of the will. As soon as speaking develops, there originates a new kind of memory. The sense impression does not sink immediately into the will sphere of the child, but is retained in the middle part of the human organisation. It touches the feelings, and in a certain way mingles with the feeling life. Thus the picture-imaginations come about. The sense impression is softened and colored by its connection with the world of feelings, just as an object mirrored

---

* According to Rudolf Steiner's teaching, which is put into practice in all the Rudolf Steiner schools in England, Holland, Germany, Switzerland, U.S.A., children should not start to learn reading or writing before the time of the change of teeth. Details may be found in Steiner's books on pedagogy.

in the waves is transformed by the softly moving water. Adults call this transformation, which they can observe working in little boys and girls, the child's fantasy. This fantasy persists naturally as long as the child still thinks in picture-imaginations. The pictures keep their life because the growth forces of the rhythmic system stream continuously into them. There are certain notable consequences if, in this period of life, the thinking is robbed of its picture character. For by the end of the third year, the growth forces have gradually detached themselves from the head organization, but are still working on the other parts of the body. A connection still exists, however, between the etheric forces of the head and those of the rhythmic and metabolic systems. This unity must to a certain extent be maintained all through life. But if there is too early a separation of picture-thinking from thinking in abstractions, this abstract thinking brings about not only a kind of paralysis of the life forces of the head, but also a general weakening of the whole human being. This condition has its repercussions on the physical body, which depends for its shaping on the inner growth forces, which are not freed until later. The resulting damage is not usually immediately visible. It becomes obvious only when the organs have used up much of their reserves of life. Only then may weaknesses of the different organs become apparent—usually in later life and in old age.

IV

Three different disturbances in human life may be mentioned in this connection. They can only be understood in the light of the foregoing considerations. Abstract thinking that is developed too early in life may lead to a hardening of the organs and a diminishing of their vital capacity. This will not be obvious before middle life—or even later. Some of the painful rheumatic diseases have their origin in the too early training of an abstract memory.*

I have said in a more general connection that through abstract thinking something hardened and lifeless becomes embedded in the organism. Now of particular importance in building up the living body is a right working together of the glands. Just consider the task of the thymus gland, which almost disappears later, while other glands have important functions throughout life. If we ask the question as to which glands could be specially affected in childhood, and much later cause the rheumatic and even sclerotic diseases, we could make a supposition that may be worth looking into. Much research has been made lately into the rheumatic-arthritic diseases, and one discovery has been made—namely, that there is a strong connection between the working of the suprarenal glands and rheumatic symptoms. Thus, it seems likely that of all the glands, the suprarenals may be specially damaged by an early training of memory. I could imagine that through the training of his powers of recollection, the child really suffers continual little shocks that disturb the suprarenals. (These are always sensitive to shocks.) In childhood there will only be slight damage, but rheumatic-arthritic-sclerotic symptoms will manifest themselves in the second half of life.

---

* Rudolf Steiner says, "One can come across people who say that at the age of forty, or later, they had shooting pains in their joints. Well, there may be all kinds of reasons for this, but there are certainly cases in which one finds, if the investigation is carried back far enough, that the rheumatism, the shooting pains in the joints, have their origin in an over-burdening of the memory in the early years of childhood."

V

Then there is another disturbance that shows itself much later in adult thinking.

Rudolf Steiner indicates that the box of bricks is a doubtful toy for children if it is given to them too early. With this toy the child is expected to build houses, bridges, fortresses and castles. The materials provided are regular, geometrical, more or less equal sized pieces of stone or wood. Very often there are also included, as plans for the construction of these buildings, a variety of pictures utterly lacking in taste.

As a result of such an occupation the imaginative power of the children suffers harm. The creative force of thought, which at this age should be a unity, is split up and atomized. The result is a onesided, analytical intellect in the grown-up. A break is formed between the mind and the feelings based on the rhythmic system. Looked at from this point of view, materialism, with its analysing, rationalistic thinking is rather an illness than a world conception worked out in freedom. What in early childhood appears undivided—the creatively and imaginatively working thinking—is broken up into little bits.

An ideal and health-bringing activity for the child, in every respect opposite to that provided by the box of bricks, is playing with a heap of sand. Everything can then be built in this. If he is given a sand-pit in his playground, the child can work with undifferentiated and undivided matter. He can imprint a form upon the oneness of the sand, in just the way that nature works on all living matter. Once one understands this, it becomes quite clear why Steiner suggests, even for the child of school age—that is, even long after the age of three to five years—the following way of teaching the beginnings of arithmetic. One should always start with a totality from which one then subtracts, or into which one divides. Neither addition nor multiplication are taught first, for in these, the whole is formed from the parts, but first come subtraction and division, that is, resolving the whole into the parts.

In his method of education, the teacher must work upon the child in the same way as nature works to develop the forces of life. If he disregards nature's example and prefers to approach the child with an analytical intellect, he will rob him of his life forces. The child will be made ill in body and mind in later life.

What happens when arithmetic is taught by the method of starting with the parts and not with the whole, Steiner describes in the following words, ". . . we sow in the child the seeds of the desiccation of the physical body, and of its sclerosis."

VI

The third disturbance we shall discuss here is closely connected with the previous one, but as we are dealing with the education from three to five, it must be thoroughly explained. The above-mentioned mistakes in education may not only give rise to a lifeless, analytical thinking, or a physical illness; it may also constitute a grave danger to the entire soul life with the result that the victim of these mistakes remains entirely without imagination for the rest of his life. What does this imply? That his head produces thoughts that have no link whatsoever with his feeling life. But is this not one of the fundamental evils of our time? The well-trained mind of a scientist is capable, nowadays, of combining matter and force in such a way that the

129

whole of humanity could be destroyed by a war. Do any of the scientist's feelings enter into this? Hardly, for intellectual work is entirely segregated from the other faculties of the human being; it is no longer a creation of the whole man, but emanates from something almost resembling an "electronic machine."

Are we not, then, in considering this, on the track of one of the true causes of that illness over which there is so much racking of brains: schizophrenia? It is certainly one of the symptoms of this mental affliction that the patient has thoughts that are in no way connected with his feelings and acts accordingly. He may perhaps kill another person by a mathematically thought-out method and feel no sympathy or remorse. The increasing incidence of certain crimes will never be explained until it is discovered that the illness of soul that has seized the criminal is the result of his early education! I must hasten to explain the particular educational mistakes I mean, in order to avoid the smiling retort that the influence of early environment on the forming of character is perfectly well-known. If, then, the life of a child early takes such a course that, through misguided playing and learning, the thinking power is torn out of its connection with the feelings, then that child will fall a victim, in *old age,* to the disease of arteriosclerosis; or in *middle life* he may develop a lifeless, analytical, and materialistic thinking power, either as a scientist or a business man or in some profession; while between the age of *twenty and thirty* he may become a schizophrenic or a criminal. This may sound extreme. But there are of course many intermediate stages that could also be enumerated.

I will give some further examples. People who are lacking in imagination find solitude intolerable. They feel themselves to be inwardly so empty that they are all the time seeking for diversion and amusement. They cannot live without cinema, radio or television. Others try to replace what they have lost in their souls through sport. What does old age bring to these people? They feel lost and alone, especially if they become bodily incapacitated and can no longer get so much enjoyment from their various entertainments. They find their loneliness unjust and torturing. One can even notice in children who are lacking in imagination that they are unable to do anything out of themselves if they are left alone for any time. This is already obvious in the first school years. Such boys and girls feel intolerably bored in the holidays when they do not have to go to school.

VII

The question arises as to what can be done in the period from three to five when the growth forces of the rhythmic system are gradually freed to avert these menacing dangers. Whatever surrounds the child must be beautiful and artistic. He should be in close contact with growing nature, with the meadows, flowers and trees. A friendly connection with animals should also be cultivated—always in a sincere and unsentimental way. It is not necessary to be always telling a child how lovely the flowers are, how sweet the dog, cat, goat, or whatever it may be. The child will have the right approach to flowers, trees and everything in nature, if he feels a reverent attitude towards them in the grown-up.

The etheric forces of the child must be given the possibility of remaining alive and mobile. It is therefore to be recommended that children should do eurythmy as soon as they are three years old. This art of movement founded by Rudolf Steiner cannot here be described, but one can learn about it from the appropriate books by Steiner and by his pupils. Children at this age enjoy making the movements. In the nursery classes of the Steiner school, eurythmy is one of the essential subjects.

From this one can see how important education in the nursery school is. The question of the nursery school has become a topical one in these days because of changes in the social life which necessitate that the mother goes out to work. During her working hours, she has to make provision for the children. In this sense, the nursery school is to be regarded as a necessary evil, which can also, of course, be turned to good. In reality it would be best for the little boy or girl to stay at home with his or her mother, if she has the right understanding.

They should learn and gain from her everything of which their souls and bodies are in need. The child will quickly learn to imitate in play all that the mother does about the house. But she should never try to "train" him. He can have his duster for polishing the floor, his little broom for sweeping, a table for cooking and a little spade and rake for the garden. All these activities must be guided in a lighthearted way with no trace of pedantry, and at the same time in such a way that the mother keeps the child in mind during her housework.

What should be done at home can also be cultivated in the nursery school with a group of children. But there should be no aim or ambition to teach children between the ages of three and seven as if they were at school. They should have nothing at all in the way of special lessons. Unfortunately, children in the Montessori kindergartens and similar institutions can already write and reckon at the age of five. Many people think that this achievement is of practical value, but as a matter of fact it kills the imaginative power, not only in childhood, but also for later life. The methods that are practiced in these kindergartens are bound to ruin all artistic feeling. At the outset of teaching, these schools make use of the "bricks and cubes of Froebel" as Montessori herself writes in her world-famous book about education in early childhood. The three year old children have put into their hands just those very things which according to the above considerations they should never touch. They are given, for instance, those inartistic toys that differ from one another only as to size. The object is to teach the child as early as possible the idea of dimension. This is only an example. Anyone who wants to know more about it need only visit one of the many homes based on Montessori education, or read the standard work of its foundress.

VIII

In these days, people like to argue about why such great value is attached to imagination in education. Strangely enough it has very many practical results.

An outstanding observation can be made in children between three and about four and a half years, of something that gives rise to many a headache in parents and psychologists. This is an obstinacy and stubbornness, which may last for some time. It can be counteracted, if it is understood rightly, out of the nature of the child's own constitution. First, whoever is looking after the child must remember that at three years, the child feels himself for the first time as an individuality. So far as the physical body is concerned, a certain harmony has been reached by the development of the sense organs, the ability to speak, the solidity of the limbs and the adjustment of the metabolism. In this harmony the child feels itself as a unity. One more fact must be added—that the forces of thinking have become to a certain extent freed from their physical and organic connections, so that the child is in a kind of way enabled by this power of thinking to look at himself, even if it is only in a simple fashion. These thoughts still occur in the form of pictures. They sink into the feeling life, which has been freed up to a point through the development of speech.

This child, then, who is capable of cultivating his thought life—a thought life imbued with imagination—can to a certain extent take hold of his will forces through this power of thinking. Imagine, for instance, a child playing with a sand-heap. He builds up all kinds of forms that to him are houses, palaces, trees and rivers. They all come out of his picture-imaginations. He goes on playing happily and peacefully. But the moment another will comes in and tries to interfere, the peace will immediately be shattered. An adult appears, for example, and cannot leave the child alone to shape the sand according to the inner imaginative pictures, but wants to impose his own ideas. This arouses the child's will to an uncontrolled response. The child defends himself and resists the influence from without. He becomes obstinate. He wants to follow his own instinctive will, and is opposed to everything and everybody outside himself. The element of thinking separates itself from the rest of the soul, and only blind resistance remains. This fury can become so violent that the child may now act in complete opposition to what lives in his ideas. He feels that these ideas, no longer imbued with imagination, come not from inside but from outside. One must realize that at this age the will is strongly tied to the body, and is chaotic and wild. An overtired child can clearly reveal this state of affairs. The influence of the sense organs and the thinking upon the feelings, with which they are usually closely connected, is gradually lost. What is the outcome? The little boy or girl, who has been playing peacefully and happily with its toys, now suddenly pulls off the tablecloth, tears down the curtains and kicks and screams without any longer knowing why. A destructive element arises out of the body.

Obstinacy between the ages of three and five indicates a kind of crisis in the child. It hardly ever appears again in the same way. The state of affairs at this time is characterized by the child's experience of the awakening ego, and also by the bondage of the will to the body. A third fact has to be taken into consideration, namely, that a kind of thinking lives in the child that is linked to the feelings by the forces of imagination so that the will is influenced by the world of feeling. If the dream-like element of imagination is lacking (as a result of feeding the child with too many abstract thoughts and ideas) then the thinking has little influence on the will and instincts. Just the opposite happens to what should be, and the unbalanced and unruly will rises up and overwhelms the middle region of man. The child protects himself against all other people, and becomes thoroughly difficult. An education that takes these urgent questions into account will never cut the child off from the realm of fantasy, and in this way can avoid or shorten the period of obstinacy.

Thus we can with good reason contradict those experienced

child specialists and psychologists who take it for granted that nothing can be done to influence the obstinacy that shows itself between the third and fourth years, but that it must be accepted as a natural occurrence.

IX

I have mentioned fairy tales so often that it may be of use to consider a few practical points in this connection. The telling of stories is important for the nursery-school age, but far more important is the right choice of tales for the period between three and five. It is necessary to consider the whole constitution of the child in these years, if one wants to find the most suitable fairy tales. I have already described the stage of development that is reached at this time. The individuality is now for the first time feeling itself at home on earth. In the soul, imagination and the power of thought are closely interwoven in a realm of pictures. This realm is akin to that from which those growth forces originate that have formed the sense organs and nerve system. Much has radiated from the world of the stars into the powers that built up these organs. Thus it is appropriate that at the age of three, the world of the stars should be presented to the child in the form of those true pictures to be found in the fairy tales. It is at this time that the formative forces are loosened in the rhythmic system from their strong connection with the physical body. The feelings then respond quite differently to, and are beneficially stimulated by, everything that comes to them by way of music and speech.

The willing soul is still working in deep slumber. But before the end of the fourth or the beginning of the fifth year, there dawns in the child the first awareness of this working will. It is now that the formative and growth forces are loosened from their ties with the metabolic-limb system. Between five and seven, when the will is to some degree freed from its physical chains, the first beginnings of a moral understanding appear in the child's mind. It is quite wrong to expect moral behavior before this age.

It is of the greatest help during the years from birth to seven to lead the child to something in the world to which it is related; related, of course, in the highest sense. The brain, for instance, is built up in accordance with influences from the realm of the stars. The child feels itself related to this realm at the time when the growth forces of the head have finished their task, and now the spiritual influence of the stars can be shown to him in true pictures.

The parent or teacher who understands this will accordingly tell the right fairy tales at the right time. The first question that present-day people will ask is: where are such fairy tales to be found as do justice to these demands? Rudolf Steiner laid much stress on the fact that the fairy tales told by the Brothers Grimm and by Bechstein are the best that we can give to our children. From among these one can select stories according to age.

Soon after three one can tell them "Snow White and the Seven Dwarfs." Why? Here is everything, given in the clearest and most impressive pictures. I shall not go into much detail here, as I have already done this in other studies. But Snow White may be mentioned as an example. The incarnation of man is described in a vivid picture: The drops of blood in the white snow, framed by the black ebony window frame. And where does the queen gaze? Into a supersensible world that she can see through the window, and where a symbol is inscribed announcing the coming of her child. In addition, we are told of a world in which the elemental beings are still full of life. The children love such pictures because they can remember their own experiences of such beings—experiences that the adults are incapable of sharing. How often can one observe children conversing aloud and sometimes laughingly with something that the grown-ups cannot see at all. One can then have the feeling that it is not an over-fertile imagination that is providing the child with so much amusement, but rather perhaps that he has come across some of those beings who appear in the fairy tales as dwarfs, and who "dig and hack in the mountain for ores."

Snow White provides another feature that is beneficial and helpful for this age especially, and that is the rhythmic element in which the children long to live. That situation, for instance, in which the stepmother asks:

> "Mirror, mirror, on the wall
> Who is the fairest one of all?"

is described seven times.

Each time a special tension is produced by the question, and each time there follows an answering relaxation. It is like the regular beating of the heart in systole and diastole.

A similar rhythm is given by the seven questions of the dwarfs, "Who has been sitting on my little chair?" etc. We experience the tension that lives in the little dwarf, and the listener himself feels the relaxation because he knows that it was Snow White, of course, who sat in the chair, tasted the vegetables, took a bit of bread, etc. We provide still another rhythm if we tell the story every day, if possible in the same words. It should never be read from the book, but always told; it is most essential that a living human being passes the fairy tale on to the child in the right mood.

In the earliest period of life, all star and sun stories are suitable, such as, for example "The Star Money."

Each fairy tale can go on being repeated for some time. The parent or teacher must rely on an inner sense to tell him when the child has had enough of Snow White, or the Frog Prince. If it is thought that the child especially needs something rhythmic, the short story of the Louse and the Flea may be interposed between the repetitions of the long one.

From these descriptions it should become clear how the life of thought may be guided in children between three and five. Another problem will also present itself—how the world of feelings should be led into the right path during childhood. One must first consider the state of development at this age. From the third year onward feeling and will are still more or less a unity. This statement gives an immediate clue, namely, that hardly any of the child's activities at this time should be considered from a moral point of view. Whatever he does is governed by the feelings of his heart. How then can we help? First by a right cultivation of the powers of speech, as above described, then by singing, music and eurythmy.

One can gradually try to develop a certain feeling of devotion—a religious feeling. If this is done in a natural way, then the will forces become freer from the fifth year onwards. Much can be achieved by example. The child should see and feel the great love that the adults have for the flowers and animals, and for their fellow men. As soon as, by imitation, he has learned to speak, a great love for all the living beings around him

139

will wake up in his soul. When the child reaches his third or fourth year, it may be a good idea to give him an opportunity to observe the animals, and perhaps even to look after one. One should be careful, of course, to make sure that the child is advanced enough to care for an animal without hurting it. Before the age of three, hardly any child can understand how painful it is for a cat, rabbit or whatever it may be, to have its fur or tail pulled. After the third year, and more especially after the fourth, one can strongly recommend letting children occupy themselves in the garden. It will be a great help for later education if the little boy or girl has learnt to plant and water flowers, or perhaps even grow some vegetables from which they can cook themselves a meal. The will is then active, and the growing human being learns to understand in time that where you work, where you dig and sow, there you are creating. Even if this is only woven into the feeling life of the child, a moral force is there formed that will become free when the will is to a certain extent liberated after the fifth year. Out of this can develop in later life a religious moral outlook, which will have its origin in man himself and not in the old traditions.

During these years, the child flourishes through its feelings of joy in everything and love for all beings. One cannot describe in general rules how this joy and love should be maintained. All depressing and painful influences should be eliminated as much as possible from the child's surroundings at this age.

Just as physical hardening in the first years (cold baths, too little clothing, etc.) is not only senseless but even dangerous and harmful for later life—so also are "gymnastics of the soul" dangerous. How often do children, in their early years, hear that they cannot have this or that because their parents have not enough money. Children should not be spoken to in this way at an early age. An understanding mother or father will overcome such difficulties in a better spirit, and by keeping the child occupied and amused in the right way. Much can be done in these years to avoid the appearance of envy and jealousy, those two evil powers that arise in many people's hearts. Again, a child should never be allowed to have the feeling that his parents have more love for a brother or sister than for himself. This jealousy can arise only if the parents show a wrong attitude. A baby who comes into the world should awaken in the three or four year old so much love and interest that he will quite happily accept the fact that the mother devotes much of her time and attention to it. The older child must be allowed to take part in the love and care that is given to the younger brother or sister. But the moment a mother or father shows greater interest in the newcomer, or perhaps makes some such remark as, "Oh but you are big enough now . . ." jealousy will all too easily take root, and work in a devastating way on the young soul. With sensible treatment of the situation, such a thing should never be possible as that a child will be goaded by jealousy to the point of putting the hand of a baby brother or sister in the fire, purely with the idea of hurting it. It is only through wrong treatment that such jealousy can creep into a child's soul. Important, too, is the necessity to avoid giving a child of perhaps five the responsibility of looking after younger ones. Such a little five year old girl will come to look already like a worried housewife. She will grow prematurely old and lose that light-heartedness of innocent childhood that is so necessary for right development of body and soul.

After the fifth year, when the etheric or life forces are freer in the sphere of the will also, the child becomes more harmonious and balanced in his whole being. From that time on, one can begin to teach him what he may or may not do; he is now more open to such teaching.

The liberation of the will forces from their strong attachment to the organic processes comes to a certain conclusion with the change of teeth.

Until the appearance of the second dentition, at the end of the seventh year, the metabolic system and its will organization are working actively right up as far as the realm of the head. The teeth themselves belong to the digestive tract and are so treated in anatomy. Nevertheless, in so far as their form and hardness is concerned, they come under the influence of the formative forces of the head organization. As soon as the working of the metabolic forces has reached such a level that the second teeth can break through, the head forces involved are freed from their organic activity and can be put to a different use; the child is now ready to learn and can go to school. He has entered on a new phase of his life.

FOR FURTHER READING
Five Basic Books

Rudolf Steiner intended these carefully written volumes to serve as a foundation to all of the later, more advanced anthroposophical writings and lecture courses.

THE PHILOSOPHY OF FREEDOM by Rudolf Steiner. "Is human action free?" asks Steiner in his most important philosophical work. By first addressing the nature of knowledge, Steiner cuts across the ancient debate of real or illusory human freedom. A painstaking examination of human experience as a polarity of percepts and concepts shows that only in thinking does one escape the compulsion of natural law. Steiner's argument arrives at the recognition of the self-sustaining, universal reality of thinking that embraces both subjective and objective validity. Free acts can be performed out of love for a "moral intuition" grasped ever anew by a living thinking activity. Steiner scrutinizes numerous world-views and philosophical positions and finally indicates the relevance of his conclusions to human relations and life's ultimate questions. As he later pointed out, the sequence of thoughts in this book can also become a path toward spiritual knowledge.

(226 pp) Paper, $5.50 #116

KNOWLEDGE OF THE HIGHER WORLDS AND ITS ATTAINMENT by Rudolf Steiner. Rudolf Steiner's fundamental work on the path to higher knowledge explains in detail the exercises and disciplines a student must pursue in order to attain a wakeful experience of super-sensible realities. The stages of Preparation, Enlightenment, and Initiation are described, as is the transformation of dream life and the meeting with the Guardian of the Threshold. Moral exercises for developing each of the spiritual lotus petal organs ("chakras") are given in accordance with the rule of taking three steps in moral development for each step into spiritual knowledge. The path described here is a safe one which will not interfere with the student's ability to lead a normal outer life.

(237 pp) Paper, $6.95 #80; Cloth, $14.00 #363

THEOSOPHY, AN INTRODUCTION TO THE SUPER-SENSIBLE KNOWLEDGE OF THE WORLD AND THE DESTINATION OF MAN by Rudolf Steiner. In this work Steiner carefully explains many of the basic concepts and terminologies of anthroposophy. The book begins with a sensitive description of the primordial trichotomy: body, soul, and spirit, elaborating the various higher members of the human constitution. A discussion of reincarnation and karma follows. The next and longest chapter (75 pages) presents, in a vast panorama, the seven regions of the soul world, the seven regions of the land of spirits, and the soul's journey after death through these worlds. A brief discussion of the path to higher knowledge follows. "Read... Rudolf Steiner's little book on theosophy—your hair will stand on end!" (Saul Bellow in *Newsweek*)

(395 pp) Paper, $6.95 #155; Cloth, $9.95 #154

CHRISTIANITY AND OCCULT MYSTERIES OF ANTIQUITY by **Rudolf Steiner.** An introduction to esoteric Christianity which explores the ancient mythological wisdom of Egypt and Greece. The work shows how this wisdom underwent a tremendous transformation into a historical event in the mystery of Golgotha. Formerly published as *Christianity as Mystical Fact.*

(241 pp) Cloth, $14.00 #662; Paper, $7.95 #33

OCCULT SCIENCE, AN OUTLINE by **Rudolf Steiner.** This work of nearly 400 pages begins with a thorough discussion and definition of the term "occult" science. A description of the supersensible nature of the human being follows, along with a discussion of dreams, sleep, death, life between death and rebirth, and reincarnation. In the fourth chapter evolution is described from the perspective of initiation science. The fifth chapter characterizes the training a student must undertake as a preparation for initiation. The sixth and seventh chapters consider the future evolution of the world and more detailed observations regarding supersensible realities.

(388 pp) Paper, $6.95 #113; Cloth, $10.95 #112

On Rudolf Steiner and Anthroposophy

RUDOLF STEINER: HERALD OF A NEW EPOCH by **Stewart C. Easton.** Dr. Easton's interest in Rudolf Steiner dates from 1934, and he has been involved in anthroposophical activities in one way or another ever since. A historian by profession, Dr. Easton brings together in this book innumerable facts and details of Steiner's life that have been previously unavailable to English readers. The result is an outstanding portrait of a unique personality that will satisfy a long-felt need.

(376 pp) Paper, $10.95 #427

MAN AND WORLD IN THE LIGHT OF ANTHROPOSOPHY by **Stewart C. Easton.** A new and revised edition of Dr. Easton's survey of Rudolf Steiner's anthroposophy. This comprehensive "textbook" complete with index includes chapters on the historical evolution of human consciousness, individual spiritual development, karma, the arts, the Waldorf school movement, Biodynamic agriculture, medicine and nutrition, the sciences, and more. Provides "the reader with an appreciation of the enormous wealth and richness of what Steiner gave to mankind. It serves admirably as an introduction to Steiner's work as a whole." *(The Book Exchange)*

(536 pp) Cloth, $21.00 #353

On Child Development and Waldorf Education

THE RECOVERY OF MAN IN CHILDHOOD by A.C. Harwood. Piaget and other modern child development researchers attempt to study the emergence of adult capacities in the child. But, as A.C. Harwood points out in this absorbing study of Rudolf Steiner's educational work, childhood is a time of *losing*, as well as gaining, capacities. Is there a connection between the loss of a childish faculty and the acquisition of an adult one? Yes, answers Harwood—in fact, a threefold connection.

There follows an insightful survey of the three seven-year stages of child development as depicted by Steiner. This is presented in connection with numerous examples and anecdotes on Waldorf education's use of curriculum subjects to support and assist this development child-man exchange. Other chapters take up specific facets of Waldorf education, such as foreign languages, eurythmy and music, and the temperaments. These lucid and literate explanations qualify this book as the most intelligent and stimulating introductory work on that unique approach to educating known often as "education as an art."
(211 pp)   Paper, $7.95 #411

EDUCATING AS AN ART edited by Ekkehard Piening and Nick Lyons. An important collection of essays on different aspects of Rudolf Steiner education written by prominent American Waldorf School teachers. The essays cover such topics as the meaning of discipline, fairy tales in the first grade, the teaching of Norse Myths, an arithmentic play for second grade, the teaching of history, and the future of knowledge. Many fine photos.
(183 pp)   Paper, $7.95 #275

TEACHING AS A LIVELY ART by Marjorie Spock. The author systematically describes the stages of a child's development from 6 to 13 years of age. The educational methods appropriate to these different periods are discussed. There are also chapters on the temperaments, the teacher, and the relation between teacher and child.
(138 pp)   Paper, $5.95 #450

THE WALDORF SCHOOL APPROACH TO HISTORY by Werner Glas, Ph.D. This important work is addressed to parents, teachers, and the general reader interested in education. It is based on ideas which have been put to the test in the classrooms of the rapidly expanding Waldorf School movement. Chapter titles include: "The History of Civilization," "In the Quest of the Images From Plutarch to Bryant," and "Seventh Grade and the Calyx of Modern Consciousness." "A careful account of one aspect of the teaching that goes on in... Rudolf Steiner schools." *(Commonweal)*
(102 pp)   Paper, $6.95 #482

SOCIAL UNDERSTANDING THROUGH SPIRITUAL SCIENTIFIC KNOWLEDGE by Rudolf Steiner. This lecture of Oct. 4, 1919, begins by considering the connections of the first three seven-year periods of child development to the faculties of Imagination, Inspiration, and Intuition. Steiner emphasizes the necessity for the teacher to give a growing child knowledge beyond the child's present mental capacity, to allow for future growth.
(20 pp)   Paper, $1.95 #639

On Health and Illness

HEALTH AND ILLNESS VOL. 1 by Rudolf Steiner. The nine lectures in this volume are part of the lectures given to the workmen at the first Goetheanum. Steiner discusses such topics as the illnesses specific to life phases, the formation of the human ear, the thyroid and hormones, treatments for mental and physical rejuvenation, the eye and hair color, the nose, smell and taste, the soul life and the breathing process, and why we become sick. The pictures of the human organism are so clear, vivid and full of insight that they should be of interest both to the layman and the medical professional.

(155 pp)   Paper, $7.95 #68; Cloth, $12.95 #174

THE ANTHROPOSOPHICAL APPROACH TO MEDICINE, VOL. 1 established by Friedrich Husemann, newly edited and revised by Otto Wolff, with contributions from eight others. This first volume of a projected four-volume medical text translated from the German and written out of the approach of Rudolf Steiner's anthroposophy will prove invaluable to medical practitioners seeking a concrete understanding of the body's relationship to soul and spirit. The readable text is also comprehensible to the interested layman. This volume includes an extensive section on developmental disorders and diseases of childhood and adolescence, followed by treatments of hysteria and neurasthenia, the polarities of inflammation and sclerosis, the biochemistry and pathology of nutrition and human metabolism, the pharmaceutical science of healing plants, and the "capillary-dynamic" and "sensitive crystallization" blood tests as diagnostic tools.

(414 pp, illus.)   Cloth, $30.00 #636

OVERCOMING NERVOUSNESS by Rudolf Steiner (Munich, 1912). Practical advice for strengthening the memory and will, and directions for overcoming nervous tension. From these exercises a new inner strength is developed making it possible for the individual to better face present social conditions.

(19 pp)   Paper, $1.50 #114

PROBLEMS OF NUTRITION by Rudolf Steiner. Steiner treats from a spiritual outlook the digestive process, vegetable and animal protein, and the effects of alcohol, coffee, tea, and milk. (Munich, Jan. 8, 1909)

(22 pp)   Paper, $2.00 #124

SENSITIVE CRYSTALLIZATION PROCESSES — A DEMONSTRATION OF FORMATIVE FORCES IN THE BLOOD by Ehrenfried Pfeiffer. This important work contains 4 drawings and 26 photographic plates. It covers the technique of producing the crystallizations, used in medical blood tests and food quality testing, and discusses different experiments performed by Pfeiffer and his co-workers.

(59 pp)   Paper, $12.95 #434

p. 134 - 135 obstinancy in 3-4 yrs.

Order Form

If you enjoyed this book and would like another copy or if you want to order one of the books described on the preceding pages, please fill out the form below and mail it to us: Anthroposophic Press, 258 Hungry Hollow Road, Spring Valley, N.Y. 10977

Name _____

Address _____

City _____

State _____ Zip _____

Book #	Title	Price	Qty.	Amt.

Postage and Handling $1.75

Total Enclosed

Please send payment in U.S. dollars with order. New York residents add sales tax.

☐ Mark X in box for UPS delivery.

☐ Mark X in box for free copy of our complete catalog.